# TREATMENT PLANNING WITH CHOICE THEORY AND REALITY THERAPY

MICHAEL H. FULKERSON, LPCC-S

# TREATMENT PLANNING WITH CHOICE THEORY AND REALITY THERAPY

*iUniverse books may be ordered through booksellers or by contacting:*

*iUniverse*
*1663 Liberty Drive*
*Bloomington, IN 47403*
*www.iuniverse.com*
*1-800-Authors (1-800-288-4677)*

*Because of the dynamic nature of the Internet, any web addresses or links contained in this book may have changed since publication and may no longer be valid. The views expressed in this work are solely those of the author and do not necessarily reflect the views of the publisher, and the publisher hereby disclaims any responsibility for them.*

*Any people depicted in stock imagery provided by Getty Images are models, and such images are being used for illustrative purposes only. Certain stock imagery © Getty Images.*

*ISBN: 978-1-5320-9472-9 (sc)*
*ISBN: 978-1-5320-9473-6 (e)*

*Library of Congress Control Number: 2020907937*

*Print information available on the last page.*

*iUniverse rev. date: 05/06/2020*

# CONTENTS

Acknowledgments ................................................................ vii

Chapter 1   An Introduction to Treatment Planning with
                Choice Theory and Reality Therapy .................................. 1

Chapter 2   Choice Theory Case Conceptualization and Reality
                Therapy Treatment Planning ............................................ 9

Chapter 3   Writing Treatment Goals and Objectives ...................... 25

Chapter 4   Writing Interventions and Formulating Treatment
                Strategies ............................................................................ 43

Chapter 5   Documentation of Progress Notes ................................. 49

Chapter 6   Case Examples ................................................................. 57

Chapter 7   Integrating Choice Theory/Reality Therapy with
                Person-Centered Planning .............................................. 69

Chapter 8   Case Conceptualization Example ................................... 85

Chapter 9   Key Aspects of Choice Theory/Reality Therapy for
                the Case of Ben ................................................................ 93

Chapter 10  Conclusion ....................................................................... 99

Appendix .........................................................................................103

About the Author ........................................................................... 109

Glossary of Key Terms ................................................................... 111

Bibliography ....................................................................................113

# ACKNOWLEDGMENTS

My hope is that this book will be a helpful resource to those wishing to incorporate choice theory and reality therapy into the principles of person-centered recovery planning. Although there have been many books written regarding a variety of topics based on choice theory/reality therapy, the information regarding the application of this approach on the topic of treatment planning has been sparse. My wish is that this book will help fill some of this void.

Many people have made significant contributions in helping me complete this book, and I would like to thank them. Kim Olver for being the first person to recognize that I had some worthy ideas regarding using choice theory/reality therapy with treatment planning. Mary Kay Lamb for helping me understand the importance of people-first language. Harold Holcomb for sharing his artistic talents in creating the illustrations located in the appendix. RiverValley Behavioral Health and William Glasser International for all the training I have been provided over the years. Without the extensive training I have received from these organizations, the completion of this book would not have been possible. Finally, I am grateful to Bob Wubbolding for his recommendations on updating the research and his other suggestions regarding how to make the book more reader friendly. This book is dedicated to the late Dr. William Glasser and J. Robert Cockrum.

# CHAPTER 1

# AN INTRODUCTION TO TREATMENT PLANNING WITH CHOICE THEORY AND REALITY THERAPY

Formerly entitled *Treatment Planning from a Reality Therapy Perspective*, *Treatment Planning with Choice Theory and Reality Therapy* is designed to be a primer for mental health practitioners desiring to write treatment plans from a choice theory/reality therapy perspective. This book provides an explanation of how choice theory/reality therapy treatment planning differs from traditional treatment planning models, which are usually based on the medical model and/or external control psychology. Examples of how to write precise and measurable treatment goals and objectives are illustrated. Treatment plans from a choice theory/reality therapy perspective have been field-tested by a clinician who has discovered how to write theory-driven, person-centered treatment plans that can also satisfy the requirements of insurance companies looking for measurable treatment outcomes.

One of my goals of writing the third edition of this book was to update it to be more compatible with the principles of person-centered recovery planning. Many additions and modifications have been made to the book, including four additional chapters. One new chapter covers integrating choice theory/reality therapy with the principles of person-centered recovery planning. Using choice theory for case conceptualization is the focus of another chapter. A new chapter with a description of how reality therapy was implemented with a case study following a detailed case conceptualization from a choice theory perspective. Finally, a new final chapter with concluding comments and tips for integrating choice theory/reality therapy treatment planning with person-centered planning.

After attending numerous trainings on person-centered recovery planning, it became evident to me that I needed to update the content of *Treatment Planning from a Reality Therapy Perspective.* I also decided to include more information on how to conceptualize a case study through the lens of choice theory. Therefore, I renamed the book *Treatment Planning with Choice Theory and Reality Therapy.* Choice theory/reality therapy has much in common with the goals of person-centered recovery planning. Both support the idea of self-determination, building on strengths, person-first language, and client-driven treatment planning based on meeting a person's needs.

Another goal was to show how to write theory-driven, person-centered treatment plans that also appeal to insurance companies. I have added new case examples to show how to satisfy the expectation of person-centered care reviewers as well as creating a treatment plan that will meet the authorization requirements of insurance companies.

The publishing company suggested that I include my justification as to why I feel qualified to write such a book. I consider myself qualified to write this book for four reasons. First, as a senior faculty member of William Glasser International, I have proven that I can provide quality training regarding choice theory and reality therapy. Obtaining senior faculty status is the highest level that an instructor of William Glasser International can achieve.

Second, currently working in the community mental health centers has helped keep me up to date and on the cutting edge of all new requirements from entities such as the Council for Accreditation of Rehabilitation Facilities (CARF) and insurance companies. I am uniquely qualified to write this book because I have learned how to write theory-driven treatment plans and consistent person-centered recovery planning principles that satisfy the expectations of insurance companies.

Third, I value the importance of writing treatment plans and documentation. From early on in my career, effective clinical documentation has been instrumental in my success. As a rookie clinician trying to prove myself, it was my ability to document and write treatment plans that drew the attention of the administrators and the physicians I was working with in an inpatient setting. Because of my treatment plans and documentation, my supervisors, administrators, and coworkers knew that I had some clue as to what I was doing despite having limited experience at that time.

Finally, I am the first person to ever write a book about treatment planning with choice theory and reality therapy. Many years ago, I remember having a discussion with one of my former clinical supervisors. I told her that I wanted to write a book about a new way of developing treatment plans that was not based on a medical model. Instead, it would be a theory-driven treatment planning approach based on choice theory and reality therapy. I wanted to write about a treatment planning approach that was based on the client's wants and needs rather than a diagnosis. I remember my former clinical supervisor telling me that I could not do this because that is not the way treatment planning is done. Of course, my former clinical supervisor's words just provided me with more inspiration to write the book.

How Treatment Planning with Choice Theory and Reality Therapy Differ from Traditional Treatment Planning

Most treatment planning books are based on the medical model and/ or external control psychology approaches, such as behavior modification. Most psychotherapists use the diagnosis as the central guidance mechanism in the development of a treatment plan. Using the diagnosis of the client, the psychotherapist uses a treatment planner to identify goals and objectives associated with the mental illness diagnosis. The expectation is that the diagnosis will provide the clinician with the information to develop an appropriate treatment plan for the client.

Treatment strategies are based on what are often highly questionable diagnoses in which a treatment team of behavioral health professionals is unable to come to an agreement regarding the diagnosis. Furthermore, since these subjective diagnoses are based on treating mental illness, the goals and objectives are often not strength based and may in fact have little to do with the client's actual presenting problems.

My purpose for developing *Treatment Planning with Choice Theory and Reality Therapy* is to provide some examples of how to develop treatment plans from more of a public health model than a medical one. The inspiration for this project was Dr. William Glasser's booklet entitled *Defining Mental Health as a Public Health Issue* (2005), where he advocates the necessity to shift from the medical model to a public health model.

According to the medical model, client diagnoses are viewed as the sources of the problem. The overemphasis on using diagnosing as a basis of treatment planning seems to foster more of an external locus of control with clients. Often these clients will perceive themselves as helpless, eternal victims. In addition to the stigma of receiving dehumanizing labels such as "bipolar," "schizophrenic," "psychotic," or "ADHD," these clients are continually receiving discouraging messages from the outside world (including the behavioral health profession) that they are incapable of being successful.

For almost twenty years, I have witnessed clients coming to my office for a first-time appointment with the belief that a mental illness diagnosis was their primary issue. They have appeared to be greatly enlightened when I inform them of how they obtained their diagnosis. Sometimes they are surprised to learn that there was not a urine test, blood test, or brain x-ray that determined their diagnoses. After explaining that most diagnoses are based primarily on symptoms reported to the therapists, I emphasize that if the behavioral symptoms diminish or disappear, the diagnosis may no longer be valid. For many clients, this information helps provide them with hope that a better life is possible.

With a choice theory/reality therapy perspective, diagnoses are viewed as a symptom of a much larger problem: an inability to form healthy, need-satisfying relationships. Therefore, a choice theory/reality therapy perspective fosters a more people-first approach in relating to clients. The diagnoses are viewed more as symptoms of the problem rather than causes. Unfortunately, those with a more limited understanding of choice theory/reality therapy sometimes have the misconception that this approach fosters victim blaming. In actuality, the reality therapist helps empower the client. The reality therapist views clients as doing the best they can with the information that they currently possess. The therapist acts as a new source of information that helps with empowering clients to have more satisfying lives.

Although mental illness diagnoses provide the benefit of a brief description of client behavioral symptoms, at times they seem to be of questionable value in treatment planning. However, the use of diagnosing in treatment planning appears to be unlikely to change. This fact does not mean that choice theory/reality therapy treatment planning cannot be integrated into the *Diagnostic and Statistical Manual* treatment planning model. A reality therapist can view the DSM diagnoses of clients as the most recognizable parts of their total behavior. Next, the reality therapist can help find quality world pictures and basic needs related to the total behaviors. Frequently, team members are at odds about a client diagnosis—and yet often in agreement about the client's unmet needs, unsatisfied quality world pictures, and out-of-balanced scales. In my opinion, this is true because I believe quality world pictures and basic needs are more definable than mental illness diagnoses.

Another advantage is that choice theory language is more conducive to developing strength-based treatment goals and objectives. Thus, it makes sense, from a choice theory perspective, to use quality world pictures and basic needs as the diagnostic schema.

One of the main problems with today's treatment planning is that many of the stated goals and objectives in the treatment plans are not based on any real conceptualization of the client from a theoretical perspective. Because the treatment planning is not theory driven, neither is the therapy. According to Jacobs (1994), counseling is most effective when it is theory driven.

## Comparing Treatment Planning with Choice Theory and Reality Therapy to Other Therapy Models

In classical psychoanalysis and traditional psychodynamic approaches, the analyst is the expert of the client's experience as well as treatment planning. The interest is limited to what is going on within the individual client. The interpretation of the analyst is what is valid. Little attention is paid to external environment or stimuli as well as the organism's response to stimuli.

With behavior modification, the behaviorist is the expert and is only interested in the stimuli and the response—but has no interest in the experience of the client. The role of the behavioral therapist is to mold the client's behavior through the use of reinforcement. Treatment planning decisions are made by the behaviorist.

The cognitive-behavioral therapist is interested in the stimuli, the client's responses, and the client's cognitive functioning. Although treatment goals are developed collaboratively with the client, the cognitive-behavioral therapist is still viewed as the expert. More recently, cognitive-behavioral therapists have become more interested in what is happening to the client emotionally as well as cognitively.

Humanistic/existential therapies take into account the client's own phenomenological perspective of the environment and the responses to outside stimuli. Both the therapist and the client are considered experts of their own phenomenological worlds. These therapies tend to view clients as having the ability to find solutions to their own problems, so that humanistic/existential therapist may have a less active role in the client's treatment planning.

Postmodern or constructivist models, such as solution-focused therapy and narrative therapy, are based on the idea that human beings create their own personal view of the world. These approaches emphasize the idea of the client being the expert of their own lives. Many of the newer approaches to psychotherapy are more symptom focused and are often comprised of specific interventions designed to address specific diagnoses. In the opinion of this author, although some of the postmodern approaches have evidence to support their effectiveness, these evidenced-based methods are much more likely to be enhanced if the practicing clinician has a solid theoretical model as a foundation for the evidenced-based intervention. Occasionally, a clinician can become so focused on treating symptoms that more global issues may be missed. This problem could be analogous to a patient with a broken leg being treated only for a sore throat.

In my opinion, a choice theory/reality therapy perspective to treatment planning takes a more comprehensive approach. Like the cognitive behaviorist, the reality therapist is interested in stimuli and all environmental conditions that might impact the perception of the client, including culture, family, religion, and economics. The choice theory perspective sees activity, cognition, feelings, and physiological symptoms as interrelated but occurring in a less sequential process than other cognitive-behavioral approaches.

Unlike other cognitive-behavioral approaches, the reality therapist does not see the client's thinking as being the primary issue. Instead, the reality therapist views the cognitions as a part of the total behavior, which is designed to reduce perceptual differences between what the client wants and what the client perceives they are getting from the external world. The reality therapist also recognizes that human beings have internal needs, especially the need for love/belonging. Thus, more emphasis is given to the importance of relationships than with most other cognitive-behavioral therapies. The perceptual differences between the quality world and the perceived world would be how a reality therapist would define a client's problem.

Similar to humanistic/existential approaches, reality therapists have an interest in how clients perceive the world around them as well as how they choose to respond to the environmental stimuli. Clients are seen as the "experts" of their own perceptions, quality world pictures, and treatment goals. Plus, there is the emphasis on the importance of relationships, which is reminiscent of Carl Rogers.

Although clients are viewed as the experts of their own treatment goals, the reality therapist has the freedom to assume a more directive role when clients lack the necessary information and skills to find solutions to their problems. This choice theory/reality therapy perspective provides a nice balance between giving clients the autonomy of being the expert of their own lives while providing them with the necessary information to cope with the unsatisfied quality world pictures.

Earlier in my career, I was really attracted to person-centered therapy. Thinking that the person-centered counseling style might be best suited for me, I read *A Way of Being* by Carl Rogers. The person-centered perspective about how to engage with clients resonated with me. Although I believed this approach was effective with some clients, the majority of my clients seemed to need more than just a trusting relationship.

Choice theory/reality therapy was able to fill in the gaps by providing a comprehensive, holistic approach that when practiced most effectively includes some of the best aspects of the other schools of psychotherapy. With an emphasis on relationships and self-evaluation, reality therapy has a clearly defined theory to support it, which makes it unique in the field of psychotherapy.

Glasser has developed a method of helping people that can be easily integrated into other methods of psychotherapy. In my opinion, the flexibility and adaptability of choice theory/reality therapy are two of the approach's greatest assets.

# CHAPTER 2

# CHOICE THEORY CASE CONCEPTUALIZATION AND REALITY THERAPY TREATMENT PLANNING

Choice Theory Case Conceptualization

Reality therapy has a solid theory to justify the counseling process. In order to practice reality therapy most effectively, a clinician needs to have a good understanding of the theory behind the process. Choice theory is the basis of reality therapy. Choice theory is the brainchild of Dr. William Glasser. Glasser and G. L. Harrington developed the method of helping people known as reality therapy. According to Dr. Glasser (1998), human beings are motivated to follow "genetic instructions," which lead to fulfillment of the basic needs of survival, love/belonging, power, freedom, and fun. In addition to having healthy relationships with the important people in one's life, having some relative balance in these need areas leads to good mental health. Although having some balance is essential for good mental health, Glasser theorizes that the intensity levels of each need vary from individual to individual.

Since adequate need fulfillment is a key to mental health, this may be an appropriate starting point for developing treatment plans. In other words, instead of using the client diagnoses as the central guidance mechanism in treatment planning, the reality therapist uses the five basic needs (survival, love/belonging, power/achievement, freedom, and fun) as a diagnostic schema and a starting point in assessing client strengths, areas of improvement, abilities, and preferences. After gathering this information, the reality therapist can more easily produce a treatment plan that is more individualized and practical.

One of our major dilemmas as human beings is that we cannot fulfill our needs directly. However, there is a more specific motivator of human behavior called our "wants" or "quality world pictures." Quality world pictures include desires and images that reflect how we want the external world to be. These pictures are the pathways through which we satisfy our internal basic needs. We have quality world pictures of important people like family and friends. A job/career might represent a pathway to a sense of power. We may have certain hobbies that give us a sense of fun or enjoyment. A favorite vacation spot may give us a sense of freedom (Glasser 1998; Glasser 2011).

The reality therapist accesses client quality worlds to gather their input for the treatment plan. Therefore, the reality therapist avoids the "expert" role of "telling the client like it is" or sending an "I know what is best for you" message. Instead, clients are perceived as the experts on the content of their own quality worlds. Of course, there may be times when clients want things that could place themselves or others in danger. In these situations, the reality therapist follows the laws and ethical codes of his or her profession by intervening to ensure the safety of the client and others who could be in danger.

As human beings, we view the world through perceptions. The information acquired through our five senses enters our total knowledge filter and is then assigned a label of positive, negative, or neutral when it enters the valuing filter (Glasser 1998).

Labeling is one of the negative side effects inherent in diagnosing (Glasser 2003). Unfortunately, labels such as "bipolar" and "ADHD" and "psychotic" become part of the client's self-concept. Frequently, children and their families will define themselves by such labels. Thus, if a person sees himself as "bipolar," he is likely to generate behaviors congruent with that particular diagnosis. The reality therapist does not emphasize the diagnosis in his/her description of the client. Rather than saying, "He is an ADHD child," the reality therapist recognizes the client as primarily a human being by saying, "He is a child with a diagnosis of ADHD" or "He is a child exhibiting ADHD behaviors." This people-first perception increases the likelihood of the therapist treating the client with respect because human beings tend to look for information to support their current perceptions.

When we perceive that we are getting what we desire from the outside world, this consistency between our quality world and our perceived world gives us a sense of need fulfillment. However, when we detect inconsistency between our quality world pictures and the perceived world, our behavioral system produces a frustration signal, which causes us to generate *total behavior* (Glasser 1998; Glasser 2011).

According to Glasser (1998, 2011), the behavior that we generate is total. Total behavior is comprised of acting, thinking, feeling, and physiology. Using the car analogy, Glasser describes the acting and thinking wheels as the front wheels while the feeling and physiology are the back wheels. Since we have more control over the acting and thinking wheels, this is the most logical place to begin when helping people make changes in their lives. These four components are inseparable; if one changes a thought or action, the other components will also change with it. In essence, acting plus thinking equals feeling and physiology. Although the impact of the change in the acting and thinking wheels may not be immediately recognizable in the feeling and physiology wheels, they will eventually come along with it (Glasser 1998; Glasser 2011).

The behavioral system generates two types of behaviors: organized and reorganized. Organized behaviors are behaviors that have been used in the past for producing need fulfillment. However, once these behaviors are no longer effective, new behaviors are created; this is called *reorganizing*. Since the reality therapist looks to build on strengths, identifying effective, organized behaviors is crucial in treatment planning. If there no effective organized behaviors are present, the reality therapist will help the client reorganize or find new, more effective behaviors (Glasser 1998; Glasser 2011).

The concepts of organizing and reorganizing are very important in terms of the practice of reality therapy. People do not change their behaviors until they recognize the ineffectiveness of the choices they are making. Consequently, people will continue with less effective behaviors while expecting more positive results. This is why the procedure of self-evaluation is such an important part of reality therapy. Once people have made the value judgment that their choices are not as effective as they would like them to be, the process of reorganizing can begin. At this time, people will entertain the idea of new ways of thinking and acting (Glasser 1998, Glasser 2011).

The total behavior that originates inside of us has a purpose. The purpose is to impact the world around us so that we get the perception that there is consistency between our perceived world and our quality world (Glasser 2011). Robert E. Wubbolding (2015a, 2015b, 2016) adds another purpose of total behavior is "to send a message to the rest of the world." When a person enters counseling, usually one component of the total behavior is more recognizable than the others. The more recognizable total behaviors will likely influence the diagnosis given to the client. Listed below are some examples:

- Acting: Disruptive behavior disorders (ADHD and ODD) and substance abuse disorders.
- Thinking: Psychotic, cognitive, and impulse-control disorders.
- Feeling: Affective disorders (bipolar and mood disorders) and anxiety disorders.
- Physiology: Somatoform disorders.

In today's managed care health system, the clinician needs to ensure that treatment goals and objectives are related to the DSM diagnoses that describe the client's total behaviors. Although reality therapists do not tend to emphasize diagnosing when working with the client, the diagnosis can be useful in summarizing many of the client's total behaviors.

In summary, human beings operate similarly to a negative feedback control system loop. For a more detailed description of choice theory, please refer to Dr. Glasser's *Choice Theory: A New Psychology of Personal Freedom.* For an illustrated diagram of choice theory, please see the appendix.

Reality Therapy Treatment Planning

Relationships are of primary importance in the practice of reality therapy (Corey 2017). One of the best ways to describe the choice theory/ reality therapy treatment-planning perspective is client focused. As stated previously, the reality therapist does not rely on the DSM diagnosis as the central guidance mechanism of treatment direction. Instead, the reality therapist relies on client input, especially input related to the client's quality world pictures.

Reality therapists clarify and negotiate their roles in helping by exploring client expectations as well as sharing their own. Reality therapists may ask, "Tell me what you would like to get from therapy. How will you know when you no longer need therapy? What would you like to see included as a part of your treatment plan? How do you see me helping you?"

Glasser (1994) identifies six things other people must know about us before we can help them:

1. Who am I?
2. What do I stand for?
3. What can you expect from me?
4. What can you not expect from me?
5. What can I expect from you?
6. What can I not expect from you?

I have found these six questions to be very helpful in establishing and maintaining boundaries with clients as well as negotiating a defining role in helping. Glasser (1994) describes four relationships: friend to friend; manager to employee; counselor to client; and teacher to student. Although a therapist primarily functions in the counselor-to-client mode, the three other roles are important in order for the therapist to effectively help the client. These six questions are especially helpful when the therapist is in the managing role. The appendix includes an example of how these questions can be used to clarify roles and expectations in the therapy relationship.

With reality therapy, the counselor-client relationship is viewed as one of collaboration in which both parties are viewed as equals. Modeling what Dr. Glasser calls the "seven caring habits" (supporting, accepting, trusting, listening, encouraging, respecting, and negotiating) is essential for the reality therapist to establish therapeutic conditions for the process to be effective (Glasser and Glasser 2000).

The reality therapist listens for perceptual differences between what the clients want and what the clients have, which can be defined as the presenting issues bringing clients into treatment. Once the presenting problems are defined, the reality therapist may take a first step in treatment planning by reframing the presenting problems into potential solutions based on uncovering the quality world pictures tied to the presenting issues. For example, the client may state, "I cannot tolerate being disrespected by my peers." The reality therapist may paraphrase by saying, "It is important for you to be respected by your peers." The client acknowledges that the reality therapist's paraphrase was correct and knows that the therapist is in tune with the client's quality world. Furthermore, there is a subtle shift in the session from a problem-focused perspective to more of a solution-focused perspective, which helps create a more positive atmosphere in the therapy session.

The reality therapist focuses on current behavior by exploring what clients are doing, thinking, and feeling—and even their physiological symptoms. These components of total behavior are not dealt with in isolation from one another. Emphasis is place on the acting and thinking components because these two dimensions are more controllable.

Reality therapists assist clients in recognizing the inseparable relationship among the four components of total behavior by connecting what the client is doing and thinking with what they are feeling and their physiological symptoms. As a result, clients gain more awareness and control over their total behaviors (Wubbolding 2017).

Just like reality therapy, treatment planning emphasizes actions. This is mainly because actions are the easiest component of total behavior to measure. Examples of ways in which a reality therapist may explore total behavior include saying or asking: "Give me some examples of how you have tried to resolve your issue," "How do you know when you are unhappy?" or "When you are feeling happy, what are you doing?"

Wubbolding (2011) describes self-evaluation as "the keystone in the arch" (2011) of the practice of reality therapy. In reality therapy, clients are continually encouraged to evaluate their progress toward treatment goals and objectives. They are also asked to evaluate and reevaluate their treatment plans. Examples of self-evaluation questions and statements include:

- "Share your perception of what goals and objectives you have achieved and which ones you have not."
- "Are your current treatment goals and objectives realistic?"
- "Is your current treatment plan working for you?"
- "How committed are you to your treatment plan?"

Glasser (1990) identified self-evaluation as the core component of reality therapy. In the appendix, you will see a diagram of the sandwich analogy used to illustrate the practice of reality therapy. Notice that the procedure of self-evaluation and the emphasis on relationships are the "buns" of the sandwich, which help to hold everything together.

The emphasis on self-evaluation and relationships is what seems to separate reality therapy from other forms of cognitive-behavioral therapy. For more information of the procedure of self-evaluation, I recommend Dr. Robert E. Wubbolding's *Reality Therapy for the 21st Century* in which he writes extensively about the different types of self-evaluation questions that can be used in therapy sessions with clients. Another recommended reading would be Wubbolding's more recent book *Reality Therapy and Self-Evaluation: The Key to Client Change*.

Action planning is less likely to be effective if the therapist skips the evaluation procedure of reality therapy. As previously stated, most people do not make changes until they have made the self-assessment that what they are doing is not working as effectively as they would like. Action planning is a central part of reality therapy. Wubbolding (2017, 2011) uses the acronym SAMIC to describe some of the major elements of an effective plan:

- simple
- attainable
- measurable
- immediate
- controlled by the planner

The aforementioned characteristics of an effective plan are very similar to the characteristics that most managed-care organizations (MCOs) are requiring for treatment goals and objectives in order to authorize treatment services. Many MCOs are using the SMART acronym for describing the characteristics of effective treatment goals and objectives. The SMART acronym stands for the following characteristics:

- specific
- measurable
- achievable
- results oriented/relevant
- time limited

## Specific

Treatment outcome measures need to be specific in that they describe when, where, what, and how the progress will be measured. The more precise the outcome measure, the easier it will be to evaluate progress. Vague treatment outcomes, such as "Client will improve self-esteem," are difficult to evaluate because progress will be based on the subjective perceptions of treatment team members. Treatment team members are likely to disagree about whether the treatment outcomes have been achieved, which makes determining the end of services much more challenging. Debate among treatment team members about whether outcome measures have been achieved is often a sign that more specific treatment outcome measures are required.

When clinicians emphasize the importance of effective treatment planning, treatment plans become valued documents, reflective of treatment, and exceed the minimum requirements for service approval. The treatment plan should be a clear road map for guiding the treatment team. Specific, individualized treatment plans demonstrate good outcome measures and client care.

## Measurable

Logic tells us that runners are more likely to finish the race if they know where to find the finish line. Likewise, clients are more likely to achieve their treatment goals if they can easily measure their progress toward achieving them. Sometimes treatment outcomes are not written in a way that is easily measured. For example, consider the two following treatment outcome measures:

1. Client will consume fruit eight out of ten times.
2. Client will consume a serving of fruit at least two times per day for a period of one week.

Which is easier to measure? Obviously, the second outcome measure is much more specific and easier to track progress.

Clearly defining progress or lack of progress will help validate the diligent work of clients and what they are doing to meet their goals. When progress is clearly defined, the treatment team can course correct, and there is opportunity to determine if the client is in the right level of care for treatment needs. Finally, measurable plans allow everyone the opportunity to celebrate steps to success—regardless of how large or small they may be.

Achievable

To write an outcome measure like "client will lose forty pounds in one week" is not achievable unless the client is planning to have surgery. Remember to assist clients in self-evaluating the achievability of their treatment goals and objectives. Unrealistic treatment outcomes can help set clients up for failure. Breaking tasks down into smaller, workable units is a way to make overwhelming obstacles more obtainable. By defining our success as taking one small step beyond where we are now, we are more likely to feel successful and less likely to feel discouraged. Please help clients develop achievable outcome measures that have a high probability of success.

Another example of treatment outcome measures that may not be measurable are those that focus totally on problem-solving. Most people coming to therapy already know the solutions to their problems. What is the solution to drinking or eating too much? Stop drinking and eating too much. What is the solution for not having any friends? Be friendlier. What is the solution to loneliness? Go out and meet people. It is more likely that people coming to therapy may be in need of thinking and acting skills to solve problems.

The ultimate goal of the reality therapist is to help clients develop skills to solve their own problems. Initially, this may puzzle some clients who are expecting to be told what to do and may ask how a skill-building treatment is going to solve the problem. My response to them has always been, "Do you want a solution to your problem—or do you want skills to solve your own problems?"

Reality therapists are information givers and/or teachers of skills. They do not put Band-Aids on gushing wounds. One suggestion would be to develop skill-building treatment plans rather than problem-solving treatment plans. Problems are not always solvable, but as clients develop skills, they may be able to diminish the size of their problems. As therapists, we may not always be able to help our clients solve their problems, but we can almost always help them develop a skill or improve a relationship that may help diminish their problems.

## Results Oriented

Research indicates that when we tell someone not to do something, we may actually help increase the probability that the person will choose to do the forbidden action (Mitchell 2009). Choice theory helps explain this phenomenon. Since all behavior is purposeful, when we focus on stopping a behavior, frustration is produced because we are taking away a behavior that has been tied to our quality world. This lack of need fulfillment produces a frustration signal, which causes us to search for replacement behaviors that are designed to satisfy the pictures in our quality world. Unless a replacement behavior can be found, we will likely resort back to the less effective behaviors we are trying to stop. Therefore, stopping without starting something new is unlikely to succeed. Instead of outcome measures like "client will stop drinking," replace it with an outcome measure such as "client will start going to AA."

In my opinion, positively stated goals increase the likelihood of success. When writing treatment plans and documenting progress, emphasize abilities rather than limitations, focusing on a person's achievements, creative talent, or skills. As reality therapists, we have to train ourselves to accomplish this task because—as choice theory explains—human beings are more aware of when their needs are not being met than to when they are being met. The human body produces frustration signals when our behavioral system scales are out of balance.

Here are some examples of negatively stated outcome measures:

- Client will reduce punching holes in walls from five times weekly to two times weekly.
- Client will reduce suicide attempts from six times annually to two times annually.
- Client will not relapse for six months.
- Client will reduce aggressive outbursts from eight out of ten times to six out of ten times.

An example of a more positively stated outcome measure would be "client will maintain sobriety for at least a six-month duration." This example of an outcome measure is more positively stated because it focuses on what to do rather than on what not to do. Positively stated goals are very much in line with Dr. William Glasser's ideas of building on strengths rather than deficits.

In 1993, the Phoenix Suns possessed the best win-loss record in the National Basketball Association (NBA). On their way to the NBA Finals that season, they faced the Los Angeles Lakers in the first round of a best-of-five series. During game 1 of the series, the Suns played one of their most erratic games of the season, which resulted in a surprise defeat for the heavily favored Phoenix team. In preparation for game 2, Phoenix coach Paul Westphal decided to have his team view the game film from game 1 in hopes that his players studying the film would help them correct their mistakes. However, the result was that the Suns played another erratic game, which resulted in back-to-back losses.

Facing elimination from the NBA Playoffs, Coach Westphal decided to have his team study a film from one of their best performances of the season against the Los Angeles Lakers. His goal was to improve team performance by focusing on their successes rather than their failures. As a result, the Phoenix Suns won the next three games to win the series and advance to the next round of the NBA Playoffs. This story illustrates how much more effective it can be to build on strengths than to focus on deficits.

Time Limited

Just imagine how much less productive the human race would be if we were immortal. Deadlines and expiration dates are essential for keeping us focused and productive. Time-limited treatment outcome measures can help our clients and treatment team members be accountable when progress is not being made. One of the reasons that managed care organizations exist has been because some behavioral health clinicians have been negligent in establishing time-limited, treatment outcome measures. Some of these clinicians have continued to seek the authorization of services by repeatedly submitting treatment requests until the funding sources eventually deny authorization. If these clinicians can be more proactive in setting time-limited treatment outcomes, it will be easier to get authorization of treatment for those who need it the most.

Failure to establish time-limited treatment outcomes often leads to the fostering of dependency relationships between clients and their service team members for extended periods of time without observable progress. After twelve months of treatment with the same therapist, if the client needs the therapist as much or more than when services started, there may be an issue with the treatment plan.

Semantics has been one of the most confusing things in treatment planning. Many people use the terms "goals" and "objectives" interchangeably. In fact, since various MCOs and reviewers may have different definitions for goals and objectives, it is usually necessary to learn the definitions of various outcome measures from each specific funding source. What the MCO is calling a "goal" may be what you would refer to as an "objective." However, to bring more clarity and reduce confusion, I prefer to view goals as the outcome and the objectives as the steps in the goal-attainment process. I see actions plans as a way to make progress toward the objectives.

In summary, we make plans to achieve objectives. When we reach an objective, we are one step closer to goal attainment. My personal definition of a treatment goal is what progress the client will have achieved by the time services are ready to end. To assist clients in making plans, the reality therapist may ask:

- What will you do today to take a small step toward obtaining a treatment objective?
- How can you be more satisfied in reaching the goals and objectives in your treatment plan?

In the practice of reality therapy, the reality therapist will encourage self-initiated plans by the client. However, many clients do not have the information or the necessary skills to develop self-initiated plans. If this is the case, the reality therapist can help them search for organized behaviors that have been successful in the past. Some examples may be asking the client:

- Tell me about a time when you were successful in a similar situation.
- Who is someone you know who has been successful in a similar circumstance?

Occasionally, clients may not have any effective organized behaviors available to them. In these cases, the reality therapist may supply information. However, the reality therapist will ask the client's permission before supplying this information. This is one example of how giving information differs from giving advice.

Plan Sheet
Name                        Counselor                        Date

## Six Steps to Making a Good Plan

1. Simple (not complicated, a small plan, not self-defeating)
2. Specific (as to what, when, where, how, etc.)
3. A "Do" Plan (a "do something plan" as opposed to a "stop doing something plan")
4. Repetitive (something you can do each day or repeat often)
5. Independent (a plan that is contingent or dependent only upon you and not upon others)
6. Immediate (a plan that can be started right away or really soon, a "now plan")

## The Five Basic Needs

1. Survival (choosing to practice good health)
2. Love/Belonging (choosing to approach others first)
3. Power (choosing to achieve something each day)
4. Freedom (choosing to be responsible and see choices)
5. Fun (choosing to promote fun each day)

---

My Plan:

_____

_____

_____

When the plan is completed, circle "yes" or "no" beside each day of the week and comment how you feel.

Day Completed? Comment/Feelings

_____

Sunday: Yes No        _____
Monday: Yes No        _____
Tuesday: Yes No       _____
Wednesday: Yes No     _____
Thursday: Yes No      _____
Friday: Yes No        _____
Saturday: Yes No      _____

_____

I choose to be responsible and commit to the plan.

Client's Signature_____

# CHAPTER 3

# WRITING TREATMENT GOALS AND OBJECTIVES

When it comes to looking at most behaviorally based treatment planning, the identified problems are clearly stated—and the objectives are measurable. However, quite frequently, this type of treatment planning is focused on symptoms and does not address the underlying treatment issues. For example, a behavioral treatment plan may address the acting component of a client's total behavior, but it may not address the quality world pictures, perceptions, and unmet needs that are tied to the total behavior.

The reality therapy treatment-planning perspective provides a more holistic approach that goes beyond addressing the symptoms of problems. As Glasser (1998) stated, "Relationships are the root of most long-term psychological problems." From a reality therapy perspective, treatment goals and objectives focus on how people can improve their relationships with others as well as themselves and more effectively meet their needs.

Before developing treatment goals and objectives, it is important to review some of the essential components of the treatment plan. Those components include symptoms and behaviors to be addressed, baseline measures, and strengths/natural supports.

The barriers to be addressed will include the total behaviors (acting, thinking, feeling, and physiology) related to the diagnoses, which will be targeted. Usually, the total behaviors that are most recognizable will be identified as the targeted symptoms. Clients with a diagnosis of oppositional defiant disorder (ODD) are more likely to have recognizable symptoms in the action component, such as fighting or truancy. On the other hand, clients with a diagnosis of mood disorder will have more noticeable symptoms in the feeling component, such as feelings of apathy or indifference. A client with a thought disorder may present less effective self-talk as a primary symptom. Finally, some clients may come to therapy via a physician referral because of some physical complaint that has no organic basis.

Baseline measures are important for establishing where the client is at the beginning of treatment in relation to the desired outcome. It is impossible to document progress accurately without some sort of starting point. For example, knowing that a client has a baseline of four hospitalizations within the past year due to suicidal behavior will provide much more meaning to a goal of a client having a period of six months of executing a safety plan to prevent hospitalization.

Since the early days of reality therapy, Dr. William Glasser has emphasized the importance of building on client strengths. Building on client strengths is the foundation of an effective treatment plan. In fact, many of the accrediting bodies of mental health agencies encourage that these be listed on the treatment plan.

SNAP is an acronym for strengths, needs, abilities, and preferences, information that could be considered in the development of a treatment plan. Listed below is an example:

> Strengths: Intelligent, articulate, and cooperative.
> Needs: Confidence and more social interaction.
> Abilities: Artistic and musical.
> Preferences: One-on-one interaction and reading.

In summary, the barriers are identified, baseline measures are recorded, and the strengths/needs/abilities/preferences are reviewed. Next, treatment goals and objectives are ready to be formulated. With mental health practitioners viewing their clients through a choice theory lens, treatment goals are related to the elements of choice theory/reality therapy.

According to Adams and Grieder (2014), there are two different levels of goals that might be identified depending upon the service setting: life goals and service or treatment delivery goals. Life goals are general outcomes that can be stated using the client's own words, such as, "I want more friends" or "I would like freedom." Service delivery goals are more specific goals, which makes them easier to track or measure.

Life goals are often vague or general statements that can be easily related to the basic needs of choice theory. In fact, to assist my supervisees in gathering input from clients regarding their treatment plans, I have added an "'S" to life goal to produce the acronym LIFE'S goal to remind supervisees to ask their clients about how they are meeting or would like to be meeting each of the five basic needs:

- love/belonging
- inner control/power/achievement/self-worth/recognition
- freedom/independence/autonomy
- enjoyment/fun
- survival/self-preservation/health

For example, the client who states, "I want more friends" is indicating that love/belonging is an area of concern. In another case, the client who reveals, "I want to have more freedom and to get people off my back" is clarifying that the need for freedom is an area of focus. This type of input into a treatment plan is what many accrediting bodies want to see when they do treatment plan reviews. It indicates more client-guided and/or family-driven services.

One of the limitations of the life goals, or the LIFE'S goals, as I prefer to call it, is that they are often not measurable. Most clients do not state their goals in measurable terms. In addition, insurance companies usually prefer that treatment goals be documented in measurable terms. In these circumstances, being able to write measurable treatment outcomes is essential to ensure authorization of mental health services. So, the client whose LIFE'S goal is "to have more friends" could have a service/treatment delivery goal of "I will be able to list the names of three new people who meet my criteria for a friendship." The client who wants "to have more freedom" may have a service treatment delivery goal of "I will be able to obtain and maintain independent housing for one year."

Treatment objectives are the measurable steps or milestones that will need to be accomplished during the process of goal attainment (Adams and Grieder 2014). For instance, the client who has a service/treatment delivery goal of "I will list the names of three new people who meet my criteria for a friendship" may have treatment objectives of "client will develop a list of criteria that meet his/her definition of a friend" and "client will demonstrate three new social skills while in the presence of therapist." The client who has a service/treatment delivery goal of "I want to obtain and maintain independent housing for a duration of one year" could have treatment objectives like "client will be able to create a budget with income exceeding expenses" or "client will have an emergency fund with enough money to cover expenses for three to six months."

In summary, one can see a clear relationship between choice theory and person-centered treatment planning. The LIFE'S goals are related to the five basic needs, and the service/treatment delivery goals are related to the quality world pictures. Treatment objectives involve a description of the total behaviors necessary to fulfill the service/treatment delivery goals.

According to choice theory, our total behaviors are tied to our quality world pictures, and it is through our quality world pictures that we fulfill our basic needs (Glasser 1998). Likewise, in person-centered treatment planning, it is through treatment objectives that we achieve our service/treatment delivery goals. Our service/treatment delivery goals are the pathway to fulfilling our LIFE'S goals.

A treatment objective for one person may be a goal for someone else. The next few pages include some examples of treatment outcomes that could serve as goals or objectives related to each of the five basic needs. These outcomes remind us that the solutions often have little to do with the identified problem. This principle also illustrates that choice theory and reality therapy are, as Glasser (2005) taught, a mental health system rather than a mental disorder system.

Self-Preservation/Survival/Security/Health: The need for air, water, food, shelter, etc. It also refers to being mentally and physically in balance.

Examples of Treatment Outcomes Related to Self-Preservation/Survival/Security/Health

1. Client will improve diet as evidenced by reducing LDL level by 25 percent.
2. Client will improve activity/exercise as measured by increasing HDL score by 10–15 points.
3. Client will lose ten pounds.
4. Client will document a 25 percent increase in activity level and maintain it for ninety consecutive days.
5. Client's lab report will show a 20 percent decrease in sodium.
6. Client's lab report will show a 25 percent increase in potassium.
7. Client will improve his/her overall score on Wellness Assessment by 10–15 percent.
8. Client will maintain current weight for at least ninety consecutive days.
9. Client will have at least seven bowel movements within one week.
10. Client will average logging at least seven hours of sleep for twenty-one consecutive days.
11. Client will express a desire to live by reporting a level of suicidal ideation that has dropped to zero.
12. Client will express hope for the future and verbalize a desire to live.
13. Client will be free of thoughts and feelings to inflict self-injury for at least seventy-two consecutive hours.
14. Client will develop a written safety plan.
15. Patient will be injury free during hospitalization for three consecutive days.
16. Client will be free of manic symptoms for two consecutive months.
17. Client will show improved mental health as evidenced by executing a safety plan to prevent hospitalization for a duration of at least six consecutive months.
18. Client will exercise for at least thirty minutes per day for one month.
19. Client will substitute water in place of soda for each meal for one week.
20. Client will make a list of the things he has control over, influence, and no control regarding each of the problem areas in his life.
21. Client will consume no more than 1,200 calories per day for three consecutive months.
22. Client will make a list of a least five things she can do to improve her health.

23. Client will substitute fruit and vegetable snacks in place of sweets for one week.
24. Client will take a fifteen-minute walk either outside or in a public building each day for one month.
25. Client will explore four thoughts and feelings that lead to feeling out of control.
26. Client will complete a smoking-cessation program.
27. Client will develop a written safety plan.
28. Client will put his fork down on the table in between each bite of food at three consecutive meals.
29. Client will chew his food ten times before swallowing in at least eight out of ten trials.
30. Client will sign and honor a contract to keep himself safe for at least twenty-four hours.
31. Within the first three counseling sessions, client will explore three precipitants of self-injurious behavior.
32. Client will make a weekly action plan to improve his health for a period of one month.
33. Client will average eight hours of sleep for at least one week.
34. Client will achieve an HDL of at least forty.
35. Client will check his blood pressure two times per day for one month.
36. Client will weigh himself each day for one month.
37. Client will replace sodas with water for a duration of one week.
38. Client will have three servings of fruit or vegetables each day for thirty consecutive days.
39. Client will take ten thousand steps per day as measured by a pedometer for twenty-one consecutive days.
40. Client will practice relaxation techniques for thirty minutes each day.
41. Client will explore total behaviors (actions, thoughts, feelings, and physiological symptoms) related to suicidal ideation within two weeks.
42. Client will be able to identify at least three reasons to continue living.
43. Client will be able to externalize anger and direct it at appropriate objects within five weeks.
44. Client will plan three activities around positive life alternatives.
45. Client will discuss his desire to stop taking his medication with his physician.

46. Client will report any thoughts of harming herself to her clinician and identify two alternative ways of coping with such thoughts.
47. Patient will keep daily behavioral records of the frequency of self-destructive behavior for two consecutive weeks.
48. Client will identify and practice at least three new alternatives for dealing with self-aggressive impulses.
49. Client will maintain a weight of at least one hundred pounds.
50. Client will identify at least two important values and unmet needs associated with anorexic behaviors.
51. Patient will identify at least one staff member whom he feels can be trusted.
52. Patient will eat three meals a day for one week.
53. Client will identify at least three cognitive distortions related to acts of self-harm.
54. Client will be able to describe how he physically/emotionally experiences his anger. He will describe at least two ways his body feels when he is not feeling angry and at least two ways his body feels during an angry outburst.
55. Client will list at least three contacts in his safety plan in case of suicidal thoughts/feelings.

Love/Belonging: The ability to connect with others, establish intimacy, or a sense of closeness with others.

Examples of Treatment Outcomes Related to Love/Belonging

1. Client will report an improved relationship with at least three important people in his life.
2. Using Pete's Pathogram, client will report a 25 percent increase in her ability to satisfy her/his love/belonging needs.
3. Client will find and identify a meaning/purpose she/he has discovered during her/his grieving process.
4. Client will report having improved relationships with her/his teachers.
5. Client will demonstrate the ability to control impulsive behavior as evidenced by zero reports of receiving in-house suspension at school.
6. Client will report having better relationships with peers at school.

7. Client will memorize the "Seven Disconnecting Habits" and the "Seven Connecting Habits of Relationships."
8. Client will demonstrate replacing criticizing with supporting others in relationships in the presence of staff in at least three different program areas.
9. Client will describe how he/she may substitute blaming with accepting others in relationships by listing five things he/she can do to show more acceptance of others.
10. Client will reduce complaining and increase ability to trust others as evidenced by giving three examples of ways she is conveying trust in others.
11. Client will be able to explain the difference between nagging and encouraging to at least two different service team members.
12. Client will show how to replace three threatening behaviors with three respecting behaviors in relating with others during family sessions.
13. Client will avoid punishing by demonstrating use of five different negotiation skills during in-home family therapy sessions.
14. Client will demonstrate how he/she can replace bribing with three newly acquired supportive behaviors during family therapy sessions.
15. Family will utilize the solving circle to resolve three family conflicts.
16. Client will report a 30 percent increase in confidence in relating to the opposite sex.
17. Client will identify having a newly formed intimate relationship.
18. Client will describe three to five times in which he/she demonstrated an ability to express affection effectively.
19. Client will complete a weekly journal for three months on his/her perception of his/her interactions with other people.
20. Client will explore the unmet needs in each of the important relationships in his/her life.
21. Client will discuss the satisfied and unsatisfied pictures of his/her relationships with the important people in his/her life.
22. Client will explore his perception of his/her relationship with each of the important people in his/her life.
23. Client will spend at least thirty minutes in a public setting one time each week for one month.

24. Client will engage in people-watching for at least fifteen minutes each week for a duration of one month.
25. Client will identify the eye color of at least three different people.
26. Client will say hello first to at least one person each day for one week.
27. Client will smile and say hello first to at least three different people.
28. Client will smile, say hello first, and include the person's name in the greeting.
29. Client will develop at least three opening statements/questions to start conversations with others.
30. Client will share at least one interesting fact about herself to each new person she meets for the next thirty days.
31. Client will identify at least three ways to say "I love you" without words.
32. Client will practice giving specific compliments during role-plays with their therapist for four consecutive sessions.
33. Client will give three specific compliments to other people within one week.
34. Client will contact a friend with whom she/he has lost contact.
35. Client will memorize the "Seven Deadly Relationship Habits" and the "Seven Caring Relationship Habits."
36. Client will identify her/his most frequently used deadly habit and make a plan to replace it with at least one of the caring habits.
37. Client will discuss at least one thing she/he can do to move closer to each of the important people in her/his life.
38. Client will memorize the characteristics of quality time.
39. Client will practice at least twenty minutes of quality time with at least one member of the immediate family for five consecutive weeks.
40. Client will use an encouraging phrase with at least one person each day for one week.
41. Client will describe a time in her life when she/he had a strong sense of love/belonging in her/his life.
42. Client will list five ways he/she is currently demonstrating caring to others.
43. Client will discuss at least three ways she/he can be a positive role model to others.

44. Client will discuss how she/he would like other people to see her/his and compare this perception to how she/he thinks they see her/him.
45. Client will develop a list of people to contact when she/he is experiencing unwanted feelings.
46. During three different sessions, client will discuss her/his progress with substituting the seven disconnecting habits with the seven connecting habits in her/his important relationships.
47. Client will describe three occasions in which she/he said "I love you" without words.
48. Client will list five to ten newly acquired social skills and demonstrate them at the next service team meeting.
49. Client will report at least a 5–10 percent improvement in a relationship with a family member or friend.
50. Client will memorize the guidelines for entering the solving circle.
51. Client will describe at least three times that she/he successfully used the solving circle to resolve a conflict.
52. Each session client will practice self-evaluating the impact his/her decisions have on his/her relationships with the important people in his/her life for one month.
53. Client will practice starting a conversation with others at least twice per day for one week.
54. Client will talk about her/his feelings of grief with (name of person) related to losing her/his husband.
55. Client will practice countering negative self-statements by completing a daily monitoring form for one month.
56. Client will be able to recognize and identify three to five conflict-resolution styles and discuss the benefits and costs of each.
57. Client will identify three qualities he/she would like in a friend.
58. Client will initiate at least one conversation each day for one week.
59. Client will identify three antecedents to disruptive behavior.
60. Client will practice summarizing every fifteen minutes for four consecutive sessions.
61. Client will be able to verbalize at least two functions of his/her anger and how they impact the relationships with the important people in his/her life.

62. Client will read a book about choice theory and identify at least three ideas he/she will use in order to strengthen a relationship.

Power/Achievement/Inner Control/Recognition

Examples of Treatment Outcomes Related to Power/Achievement/Inner Control/Recognition

1. Client will have increase self-worth, self-control, and self-esteem as evidenced by increasing self-concept questionnaire survey score from 24 to at least 61.
2. Patient will increase his/her participation in milieu activities as evidenced by completing all assigned duties for one week.
3. Client will replace impulsive behavior with memorizing four simple questions to ask himself/herself to make effective decisions.
4. Client will improve task completions by finishing three achievement plans.
5. Client will obtain GED.
6. Client will maintain on-task behavior and will engage in thoughtful (versus impulsive) decision-making as evidenced by using the WDEP (What do you want? What are you doing? Evaluate: Is it working? Plan: What can you do differently?) questioning process with at least three people on three different occasions.
7. Client will report having a relative perception of self and demonstrate behavior consistent with adequate self-esteem as well as exhibit less preoccupation with his own appearance.
8. Client will maintain passing grades in each of his/her courses for at least one semester.
9. Client will be able to identify his/her feelings of anger in at least three different program areas when prompted by staff.
10. Patient will demonstrate by his actions that he is able to remain nonviolent when reporting feelings of anger on three different occasions as reported by staff.
11. Patient will achieve and maintain remission of hallucinations and delusions for a period of at least ninety consecutive days.

12. Client will eliminate physical aggression for a duration of ninety consecutive days.
13. By using a Subjective Units of Distress Scale (SUDS), client will report a 50 percent improvement in his ability to manage anxiety.
14. Patient will be oriented to name, place, and time for at least three consecutive weekly sessions.
15. Client will eliminate constant depressive state for a period of at least thirty days.
16. Client will show improved anger-management skills by replacing aggressive outbursts with nonaggressive conflict resolution skills for a period of twenty-one consecutive days.
17. Using Pete's Pathogram (Peterson 2008), client will show a 15 percent improvement in his/her ability to satisfy his/her need for power/achievement/self-worth.
18. Client will show improvement with his/her ability maintain focus and manage his/her emotions nonviolently for a duration of seventy-two hours.
19. Client will memorize at least five elements of a good plan.
20. Client will commit to at least one action plan per week for a duration of one month.
21. In each session, client will identify two areas of achievement and one area to be improved for a duration of one month.
22. Client will share her three greatest achievements in her professional and personal life.
23. Client will identify at least three to five things he/she could do that would give him/her a sense of achievement.
24. Client will develop an action plan without the assistance of his/her therapist.
25. Client will follow through with three achievement plans within one week.
26. Client will completely revise and update his resume.
27. Client will make at least three job contacts per week for a duration of at least one month.
28. For a history class, client will read each textbook chapter three times.
29. For one week, client will remember to bring a pencil and paper to each class.

30. Client will invite three people to join his/her weekly study group.
31. Client will prepare a practice test before each exam for one semester.
32. Client will complete a task that she/he has been putting off within thirty days.
33. Client will stay on task for least fifteen minutes for three consecutive weekly play therapy sessions.
34. Client will list twenty-five of her/his positive attributes (five in each category: physical, emotional, behavioral, intellectual, and environmental).
35. Each day for fifteen minutes, client will practice one technique that might improve her/his job skills for twelve out of fourteen days.
36. Client will identify three sources of anger.
37. Client will develop an action plan to cope with each anger source.
38. Client will practice at least one new relaxation technique during each session for six weeks.
39. Client will use behavioral rehearsal to practice assertion skills at least one time per session for six weeks.
40. Client will attend ninety AA meetings in ninety days.
41. Client will complete a twelve-week choice theory focus group.
42. Client will maintain sobriety for at least three consecutive months.
43. Client will describe his/her total behavior when recalling a time when he/she felt successful.
44. Client will describe his/her total behavior on an occasion when he/she visualized himself/herself as being successful.
45. Client and his/her therapist will explore his/her social/situational anger sources. Client will identify/verbalize at least five anger sources.
46. Client and his/her therapist will discuss anger-management techniques. He/she will acquire at least three to five new ways to effectively manage his/her anger. He/she will be able to verbalize and demonstrate at least three to five newly acquired skills to his/her therapist.
47. Client will memorize four simple questions to ask himself/herself to help remember to use his/her coping skills.
48. Client will read a book about choice theory and describe three ways he/she can improve the quality of his/her life.

Freedom/Independence/Autonomy: The ability to move and choose or to stand on one's own feet.

Examples of Treatment Goals Related to Freedom/Independence/ Autonomy

1. Client will increase her/his level autonomy, freedom, and independence by obtaining a driver's license.
2. Client will become more self-sufficient by holding a job for at least six months.
3. Client will demonstrate ten new coping skills to manage his/her emotions.
4. Client will report improving her/his self-talks.
5. Client will embrace fifteen minutes of solitude time each day for a period of thirteen weeks in order to improve her/his mental health.
6. Client will be able to develop his/her own achievement plans.
7. Client will be able to sleep in his/her own bed.
8. Client will draw three alternate strategies for managing her/his anxiety.
9. Client will develop sufficient computers skills to obtain employment.
10. Client will accept more responsibility for his/her actions by replacing his three favorite excuses with "I statements."
11. Client will demonstrate the ability to rethink rather than react by teaching the questioning process of reality therapy to at least three different people.
12. Client will improve independent decision-making skills by reporting three different occasions in which he/she resolved conflict without violence.
13. Client will be able to resist negative peer pressure for a period of three months as reported and documented by client and service team.
14. Client will learn to self-evaluate, self-monitor, and self-regulate his/her behavior by graduating an anger-management program.
15. Using Pete's Pathogram (Peterson 2008), client will report at least a 12 percent increase in her/his ability to fulfill her/his need for freedom/ autonomy/independence.
16. Using a Subjective Units of Distress (SUD) scale, client will report a 25 percent improvement in managing her level of anxiety.

17. Client will show improved mental health as evidenced by having a Child PTSD Symptom Scale (CPSS) score no higher than 14.
18. Client will identify the rules she/he lives by.
19. Client will develop a list of rules and consequences to be followed at home.
20. Client will write a list of things he/she feels he/she has to do or should do and then write a new list replacing each "have to" and "should" with "choosing" or "I want."
21. Client will list things she/he does not have to do or want to do. She/he will then shed the list and make a commitment to focus on a new list comprised of the things she/he feels she/he has to do or wants to do.
22. Client will identify three things she/he does not like about herself/himself and then name at least one positive about each thing.
23. Client will give himself/herself permission to feel unhappy for fifteen minutes each day and then will make an action plan to help himself/herself feel better.
24. Client will self-evaluate the positive choices she/he has made the previous week during each session for six consecutive weeks.
25. Client will be able to develop an action plan without the assistance of someone else.
26. Client will allow herself/himself thirty minutes of downtime each day.
27. Client will identify his/her top three excuses that prevent him/her from becoming more independent in decision-making.
28. Client will describe his/her total behavior regarding activities and places that give him/her an added sense of freedom and independence.
29. For a duration of three weeks, client will practice a new conflict-resolution skill (in role-plays with therapist) to give her/him new choices in handling disagreements with others.
30. Client will track his/her daily angry outbursts on a monthly calendar.
31. Client will describe how her/his medication impacts her/his actions, thoughts, feelings, and physiology.
32. Client will complete a trauma narrative regarding past abuse and identify three things she/he has learned from the experience that will benefit her/him in the present and future.

Fun/Enjoyment: To increase level of fun/enjoyment in ways that do not lead to getting in trouble. Learning something new can also be part of this need.

Examples of Treatment Outcomes Related to Fun/Enjoyment

1. Within two weeks, client will report an increased level of enjoyment by taking a vacation.
2. Client will replace feelings of boredom with enjoyment for a period of two weeks by reporting three things he/she accomplished that brought him/her a sense of joy.
3. Based on self-report, the client will be able to entertain himself/herself for thirty days without depending upon others.
4. Client will increase pathways for putting fun into his/her life by identifying three places to go for enjoyment that are legal and not harmful to himself/herself or the significant people in his/her life.
5. Client will increase ability to see humor by identifying three areas of his/her life that he/she is taking too seriously.
6. Client will identify a total of at least ten new ways of having fun at home, work, and community.
7. Client will demonstrate at least five new fun-making skills while in the presence of counselor.
8. Client will practice five new ways of having fun that are legal while in the presence of staff.
9. Client will list three new ways to gain a sense of enjoyment without the assistance of drugs as reported by client.
10. Client will memorize the characteristics of quality time.
11. Using Pete's Pathogram (Peterson 2008), client will show at least an 18 percent improvement in her/his ability to satisfy her/his need for fun/enjoyment.
12. Client will show improved ability to combat depression as measured by at least a 5 percent improvement on her/his Beck Depression Inventory (BDI) score.
13. Client will list and discuss five ways she/he is currently meeting her/his need for fun.
14. Client will identify at least three things she used to do for fun that she wishes she was still doing.

15. Client will identify at least three new ways of putting fun into her life without getting in trouble.
16. Client will invite a friend to do something fun each week for four weeks.
17. Client will find at least one new hobby and give himself thirty to sixty minutes each week to engage in the hobby for one month.
18. Client will discuss at least one way he has experienced fun by himself each week for thirty days.
19. Client will discuss at least one way he had fun with others each week for a duration of twenty-one days.
20. Client will start a joke file and collect at least ten jokes.
21. Client will learn at least three to five magic tricks to show others.
22. Client will make a plan to do something fun in each of his environments (home, work, church, etc.)
23. Client will read the newspaper each day for one week.
24. Client will complete an educational course of her/his choosing within the next six months.
25. Client will attend weekly guitar lessons for thirteen weeks.
26. Client will complete reading a self-help book and discuss three to five things he/she learned or relearned.
27. Client will make a list of at least twenty things he can do for fun that will not lead to trouble.
28. Client will identify three less effective self-talk statements that prevent him/her from enjoying life more fully.
29. Client will replace less effective self-talk statements with at least three more effective self-talk statements.

In writing treatment goals/objectives related to the basic needs, please keep in mind that the basic needs overlap. Therefore, a single objective may be related to more than one quality world picture as well as more than one need. The only time we can separate the basic needs is when we teach them.

Please remember to develop the treatment plans with the clients. It is essential to have the client present in order for the plans to be truly client-focused plans. What might be a goal for one client may be better written as an objective for another. Remember that the goals are the outcome of therapy, and the objectives are the process for achieving it.

# CHAPTER 4

## WRITING INTERVENTIONS AND FORMULATING TREATMENT STRATEGIES

Treatment objectives are frequently confused with treatment interventions. While treatment goals and objectives are stated in terms of what a client is going to do, interventions describe how the counselor/therapist will assist the client. Listed below are some examples of interventions a therapist may use to assist a client. Notice that these interventions are categorized into the four components of total behavior.

Activity

1. Exploration of actions
2. Assessing level of commitment
3. Action planning
4. Assertion training
5. Conflict resolution
6. Systematic desensitization
7. Modeling
8. Behavioral rehearsal
9. Relaxation training
10. Allowing natural consequences
11. Imposing logical consequences
12. Envisioning

13. Invivo mastering
14. Safety planning
15. Successive approximations

## Cognitive

1. Assessing locus of control
2. The mirror technique
3. Prioritizing goals
4. Reframing
5. Positioning
6. Restraining
7. Predicting relapse
8. Challenging less effective self-talk
9. Guided imagery
10. Cognitive processing and restructuring
11. Cost/benefit analysis
12. Coping cards
13. Psychoeducation

## Affective

1. Reflection of feeling
2. Reflection of meaning
3. Empathic responses
4. Empty Chair technique
5. Dialogue of polarities
6. Affective modulation

## Physiological

1. 1. Biofeedback

Miscellaneous

1.  Silence
2.  Simple minimal verbal response
3.  Accenting
4.  Paraphrasing
5.  Reflection
6.  Summarization
7.  Exploration
8.  Questioning
9.  Confronting
10. Educating
11. Immediacy
12. Use of humor
13. Storytelling
14. Play therapy
15. Role reversal
16. Contracting
17. Focusing
18. Funneling
19. Clarifying
20. Assigning homework
21. Bibliotherapy
22. Negotiating
23. Accepting
24. Active listening
25. Supporting
26. Trusting
27. Respecting
28. Journaling
29. Evoking
30. Affirming
31. Suggesting
32. Assessing

33. Limit setting
34. Informing
35. Teaching
36. Instructing

Behavior Management Planning

Many mental health providers are required to write treatment interventions. Traditionally, interventions have been based on the carrot-and-stick external control philosophy of behavior modification in which it is believed that if one provides the proper stimulus, a person will elicit a desired response. Usually, these approaches utilize praise or rewards for "good" behavior and criticism or punishment for "bad" behavior.

Although these approaches can be quite effective for producing temporary compliance, they do little to promote cooperation and intrinsic motivation.

Before deciding on an intervention for a client, I think it is important to ask ourselves about our goals for this particular client. Are we looking for cooperation or temporary compliance? What message will be encouraging or teaching with our interventions?

The problem with punishment/criticism is that it only teaches "Don't misbehave because you might get in trouble." The client learns to be sorry for getting caught rather than learning about the impact his/her behavior has on others.

Rewards and praising seem to teach "Do something positive because other people will like you and may give you things." This frequently leads the client to develop conditions of worth and become overly dependent upon approval from others.

Perhaps there is another method for determining interventions that encourages cooperation and learning self-respect using less controlling and noncritical methods. This approach is based on Dr. William Glasser's choice theory. The choice theory approach to developing treatment interventions goes beyond focusing on antecedents, behavior, and consequences. I have formulated a description of how this approach could be implemented using the first seven letters of the alphabet.

- Antecedents. What activating events led to the targeted total behaviors?
- Behaviors. What components are most recognizable? What interventions have been used to manage the targeted total behaviors?
- Consequences. What are the results of the targeted total behaviors?
- Determine the goal of the targeted behavior. What quality world picture is tied to the targeted total behaviors?
- Evaluation. What interventions have been effective or ineffective?
- Find a more effective intervention. What interventions may work best?
- Goal. Assist the client in setting a new treatment goal and objectives.

## Writing Reality Therapy-Based Interventions

One useful idea to keep in mind when treatment planning with choice theory and reality therapy is to distinguish theory from practice. When conceptualizing clients, use the language and concepts of choice theory (basic needs, quality world pictures, perceived world, total behaviors, etc.). On the other hand, use procedures of reality therapy when discussing interventions. Here are some examples of writing reality therapy-based interventions:

- Therapist will establish an environment that is conducive to change and build a trusting relationship with the client by using seven caring habits (supporting, accepting, trusting, encouraging, respecting, negotiating, and listening).
- Therapist will assist client with setting goals by exploring expectations of services.
- Therapist will use the reality therapy procedure of evaluation to assist the client in setting realistic goals and making value judgments regarding prioritizing goals and behavioral effectiveness.
- Therapist will provide information regarding the elements of effective plan-making to assist the client in being more focused on process than outcome.

- Therapist will implement paradoxical techniques to assist the client in reframing failure as a potential success.
- Therapist will help client reduce anxiety levels by helping him/her clarify goals.
- Family therapist will teach the client and family how to properly execute the solving circle (Glasser 1998).
- Therapist will assess the client's level of commitment to making some new changes in order to help increase client psychological flexibility.
- Therapist will use therapeutic games to show how important having fun is in building relationships and learning new things.
- Therapist will present the four-wheels game to teach the client that acting, thinking, feeling, and physiological symptoms are inseparable.
- Therapist will encourage client to journal his/her actions, thoughts, feelings, and physiological symptoms, so that he/she may become more aware of each component and gain more effective control over what he/she thinks and does.
- Using role-play demonstrations, therapist will teach client new conflict-resolution skills so that he may relate more effectively to the important people in his life.

Interventions are important because these are the services the therapist is getting paid to provide. Without documenting interventions, the therapist may appear to be assuming a passive role in the providing of therapeutic services. For more information on writing treatment interventions using a person-centered planning approach, please see chapter 7.

# CHAPTER 5

# DOCUMENTATION OF PROGRESS NOTES

Looking back at my graduate-level training in counseling and my supervision of students, I believe that training in treatment planning and documentation were underemphasized. Since much of the work of mental health professionals occurs behind closed doors, the only evidence of our work that others may see is our documentation. Poor documentation can often be a reason for mental health professionals to lose jobs or have their licenses suspended.

Document Just the Facts

Although writing opinions and critiques can provide interesting discussion and be entertaining, these have no place in the clinical progress note. Suspending judgment is the best frame of mind to be in when writing an objective clinical progress note. In choice theory terms, this kind of objectivity requires viewing clients from a low perception. Wubbolding (2017) has written that low-level perceptions are perceptions where we merely recognize the world around us. In contrast, high-level perceptions involve placing a value on it that could be positive, negative, or neutral.

Here are a couple of examples of opinions documented in a chart:

- "He was depressed today."
- "He is disinterested."

Here is how to turn these observations into facts:

- "He stated that he felt depressed today."
- "He appeared disinterested as evidenced by his withdrawal from the activity."

## Document What is Relevant to the Treatment Outcomes

Occasionally, clinicians can get sidetracked by focusing too much on irrelevant details that what eventually is documented in the progress note is a highly inaccurate picture of what actually occurred in the session.

I remember an insurance company contacting me one time because of concerns over chart documentation by a community-support associate. The issue arose because the community-support associate was a little too preoccupied with details such as where he took the client and what they had for lunch. Based on the documentation in the chart, the insurance representative got the impression that much of the service involved taking the client to McDonald's and to the mall to "pick up chicks." In reality, the community-support associate failed to give himself credit for all the therapeutic work he did because he did not document much of it in his progress note. Fortunately, after some phone conferences with the insurance representative, it was clear that the community-support associate was providing high-quality therapeutic interventions. He just did not give himself credit because it was not in the progress note.

Documentation is also important for tracking progress toward reaching treatment goals and objectives. Treatment plan should be reviewed each session. The progress note is a report on what progress has been made toward the treatment objectives and goals.

I learned acronyms like SOAP (subjective, objective, assessment, plan) and DAP (data, assessment, plan) when I was in graduate school. Although these acronyms are helpful, I have put together my own acronym because it helps to remember the importance of including documentation of the goals for the sessions as well as the interventions. Generally, mental health professionals do a pretty good job of documenting what their clients say and do. Where they are more likely to come up short is in documenting their interventions. It is just as important for the clinician to document how they helped the client as it is to document clients' observed symptoms. My own acronym is GDIP.

GDIP is a simple acronym used to remember the elements of effective documentation:

- Goal: Identify the purpose of the session, including what the helper hoped to accomplish.
- Data: Describe the dimensions of the client's total behaviors that are most recognizable, including actions, cognitions, emotions, and physiological symptoms.
- Interventions: Document the actions the helper took to help the client.
- Progress: Note progress made toward treatment goals and objectives.
- Plan: Write the plan for the next session.

Use Action Words to Describe Interventions

Listed below are some examples of some good verbs to employ when describing interventions:

| | | |
|---|---|---|
| Acknowledged | Elicited | Normalized |
| Addressed | Empathized | Provided |
| Affirmed | Engaged | Recommended |
| Asked | Established | Redirected |
| Asked | Examined | Reflected |
| Assessed | Explained | Refocused |
| Assisted | Facilitated | Reframed |
| Built rapport | Focused | Reviewed progress |
| Clarified | Guided | Set limits |
| Commended | Identified | Validated |
| Developed | Informed | Verbalized |
| Directed | Inquired | |
| Discussed | Modeled | |

Example 1

The goal of today's session was to explore and clarify client's expectations of services. Paul stated that he was referred for services due to experiencing severe depression and depression-related feelings like apathy and indifference. According to Paul, his depression has had a negative impact on his relationships at home and at school. Counselor used open-ended questions to explore client's perception of the type of help he needs and to negotiate a role in helping the client. Paul stated that he needs a "coach" to help him get back on the right track. He continued by saying he would like to understand what is causing his depression and how to effectively deal with it. Counselor assured client that he could be of assistance to him. Some progress noted regarding client being able to express his unmet needs more assertively. Next session will focus on helping client explore the connection between his thoughts/feelings and unmet needs.

Example 2

The goal of today's session was to teach Maria some new techniques for managing anxiety. At the beginning of the session, Maria rated her anxiety level as a 9 on a 0–10 scale with 10 being the highest. According to the client, accompanying her feelings of anxiety were physiological symptoms (muscle tension and a mild headache) and thoughts of "wanting to avoid all the stress in her life." Therapist taught Maria the relaxation technique of stomach breathing (to replace chest breathing) and guided imagery to cope more productively with less effective self-talk. By the end of the session, client reported that her anxiety level had reduced to a 4 on the 0–10 scale. Some progress noted regarding client learning more effective coping skills. Next session, therapist and Maria will address improving self-talks.

Example 3

Ralph began the session by reporting that he is feeling highly discouraged following his relapse after a three-month period of sobriety.

According to Ralph, he believes his relapse was triggered following several job turndowns. Client indicated that he feels like a "complete failure" for having relapsed following three months of sobriety. The goal of this session was to assist Ralph in reframing failure as a potential stepping-stone to success. Therapist used reframing to help Ralph recognize that three months of sobriety is at least a partial success and that occasional relapses can be an expected part of recovery. To cope with his perceived trigger for the relapse, therapist used reframing by helping the Ralph see that with each turndown, he is one step closer to finding the right job. By the end of the session, the Ralph reported feeling somewhat encouraged. Next session, therapist will provide Ralph with information on how to use the elements of effective plan-making strategies to put distance between relapses.

The reader may have noticed that in the documentation examples, I used first names rather than referring to the receivers of treatment as "clients" or "patients" as I was trained as a counselor. The reason for this change is to create more person-centered documentation. The practice of using the first name is also recommended for treatment planning.

Example 4

During this initial session with Martha, therapist explored expectations of treatment. Martha stated that she wants to "make her daughter behave." Therapist focused on previous attempts of Martha to change her daughter's behaviors. Martha shared that she has invested a tremendous amount of energy in trying to change her daughter's behaviors, including yelling at her a reported thirty times per day. After Martha made the self-evaluation that her previous efforts did not work, therapist used the analogy of "looking for lost car keys in the same place repeatedly" as a metaphor to illustrate how human beings have a seemingly undying belief in things that do not work. Therapist also asked Martha to evaluate the direction her behavior is taking her. Martha predicted that she will develop serious physical ailments if changes are not made. Therapist introduced the "fork in the road" analogy to illustrate that Martha has two options: maintaining her same behavioral direction or doing something different. Martha acknowledged that she is willing to try something different. The next session will focus on alternative behaviors for managing the daughter's behavior.

Hypothetical Example of a Crisis-Intervention Note

Client: Jackson

The goal of this session was to assess the lethality of Jackson's suicidal ideation and his ability to cope with the recent loss of his spouse. Jackson reported feeling depressed, worthless, and lonely. Accompanying these feelings were thoughts of suicide and pessimism. Although he does not have a history of suicide attempts or a concrete plan, he reports feeling confident in his decision to take his own life.

Jackson's negative symptoms seem to be related to an unmet need for love/belonging that has gone unmet since his wife passed away. He reports his wife as being his only connected relationship. Without a sense of belonging or a connection in his life, Jackson states that he sees life as meaningless.

To explore the purpose of Jackson's threat, therapist asked Jackson what he expected to happen when he told his therapist about making a decision to kill himself. Jackson acknowledged remembering the discussion from the initial session about the duty to warn and protect as well as the limitations of confidentiality. He also acknowledged that he suspected his therapist would be legally and ethically obligated to intervene. Following this gentle confrontation, Jackson agreed that he has some ambivalence about wanting to live or die. Therapist used self-evaluation questions to help Jackson examine the connection between his desires and behavior. Jackson made the self-assessment that it would be in his best interest to delay carrying out the decision to take his own life.

Jackson agreed to develop a safety plan. He also agreed that the therapist refer him to a crisis stabilization unit. Therapist will contact the crisis stabilization unit therapist to arrange a transition-planning conference next week

Safety Planning

For many years, no-suicide contracts were a standard practice in handling suicidal threats and behaviors. In more recent times, there has been a shift from no-suicide contracts to safety planning. Safety plans have many of the necessary elements to help ensure someone's safety.

First, most safety plans have a section on the safety plan to identify warning signs. One of the unique ways a reality therapist may list the warning signs is by categorizing them into total behaviors. Occasionally, it may be helpful to remind clients that the acting warning signs are usually the signs of which they are least aware—and they may sometimes need help from others in recognizing and understanding them. On the other hand, the warning signs categorized under feelings may sometimes be their best friends because they are usually the first signs they notice when their scales are out of balance.

Second, the "coping strategies" section provides information to help determine some of the organized behaviors that have been effective for clients as well as new strategies and/or behaviors that may help in the future. Having this information documented and visible to clients helps make the information easier for them to access in times of an impending crisis.

Third, the safety plan includes a place for ideas about how to create a safe environment. Any environmental change that can prevent access to a weapon, drugs, or other means reduces lethality.

Finally, I believe one of the most important sections of the safety plan is the "Things That Are Important to Me" list. In this section, clients list the things they feel are most important to them and that are worth living for in the future. Frequently, those who may be exhibiting suicidal behaviors are ambivalent about whether to continue living.

As choice theory explains, human beings are more aware of when their quality world pictures are unsatisfied than when they are satisfied. Therefore, we can sometimes become so focused on negativity that we forget about the blessings in our lives. The "Things That Are Important to Me" list can help clinicians begin to access client quality world pictures, which helps get them in touch with the part of the client that still wants to live. Plus, the "Things That Are Important to Me" list is a good assessment tool. If a client cannot come up with anything to put on this list, lethality greatly increases.

# CHAPTER 6

## CASE EXAMPLES

Client 1: Walter

Walter, a seventeen-year-old male, has been diagnosed with a social anxiety disorder. His parents have referred him for treatment due to his extreme shyness. He reports feeling very lonely and complains of not having any friends. His relationship with his parents appears to be pretty good. Walter seems to have a clear preference for introversion and admits that his mother or father usually act as his "spokesperson." Although Walter appreciates being the only child, he sometimes gets annoyed with his mother always "being in my business" and making decisions for him.

Treatment Plan

Name: Walter
Therapist: Mike Fulkerson, MAE, LPCC, CT/RTC
Strengths: Supportive family and desire to cooperate with others
Needs: Social skills, confidence, and friends
Abilities: Articulate, intelligent, and insightful
Preferences: One-to-one interaction, writing, and reading
Input from client: Walter states that he wants to overcome feelings of loneliness.
Barriers: An inability to establish and maintain friendships. Walter reports a high level of anxiety around other people. He reports avoiding approaching other people first for fear of rejection and avoids making

eye contact. Walter reports feeling lonely and having zero friends at school and at home. Social anxiety disorder is his diagnosis.

Life Goal 1: "I want to overcome my feelings of loneliness."

Treatment Goal: "I will connect with other people by being able to identify the names of at least three people who I consider to be a friend."

Objective 1: Walter will spend at least thirty minutes in a public setting one time for at least two consecutive weeks within one month based on self-report.

Objective 2: Walter will engage in people-watching for a minimum of fifteen minutes for at least two consecutive weeks within two months based on self-report.

Objective 3: Walter will identify the eye color of at least three different people within three months based on self-report.

Objective 4: Walter will say "hi" first to at least three different people without the expectation of his greeting being returned within four months based on self-report.

Objective 5: Walter will develop at least four questions or statements to begin conversations within five months as monitored by counselor.

Interventions: Individual therapy will occur one time per week. Relaxation techniques, assertion training, action planning, successive approximations, behavioral rehearsal, and cognitive processing will be used to assist Walter in developing new social skills.

One of the important ideas to remember in treatment planning is to keep it as simple as possible. Also, it is important to remember to start where the client is—and not where you are. If the therapist suggests that a very shy client like Walter just go out and meet people, this suggestion would be very foolish. Walter does not yet have the skills to be successful with this task. The therapist helps Walter take baby steps, which will be less likely to set Walter up for failure. Effective treatment planning provides clients with a high probability of success.

Client 2: Tonya

Tonya is a thirty-year-old female who has been diagnosed with bipolar disorder. Her mother has custody of Tonya's child due to Tonya's instability in relationships and with holding onto jobs. Tonya reports that she has noticed increased feelings of depression because she has not been able to find a job. She says that she feels very discouraged and is at a loss as of what to do. Tonya has a history of having poor relationships with her work supervisors and has not been able to hold a job longer than three months. She blames having poor supervisors for her inability to keep jobs.

Treatment Plan

Name: Tonya
Therapist: Mike Fulkerson, MAE, LPCC, CT/RTC
Strengths: Extroverted, outspoken, demonstrative
Needs: Conflict-resolution skills and increased internal locus of control
Abilities: Creative and resilient
Preferences: Visual learner
Barriers: Instability at work and in relationships. Tonya has been unable to hold a job for longer than three months and has made very few job contacts.
Life Goal 1: "I would like to maintain a job by learning how to get along with difficult people."

Treatment

Goal 1: "I will be able to maintain a job for at least six months regardless of how difficult my coworkers are to get along with."
Objective 1: Tonya will report to therapist making at least three job contacts per week for a duration of least six weeks.
Objective 2: Tonya will memorize four simple questions to ask herself to help her remember to use her coping skills within thirty days as monitored by therapist.
Objective 3: Tonya will be able to identify and demonstrate at least three new conflict-resolution skills in the presence of her therapist within the next ninety days.
Interventions: Individual therapy will occur one time per week. Therapist will assist Tonya in learning to reframe her perceived failures as

stepping-stones to success. Therapist will also teach Tonya how to use the questioning process of reality therapy as a self-help method. Role-plays will be used to teach conflict-resolution skills.

Client 3: Juan

Juan is a seventeen-year-old male who was referred for treatment by his mother. She reports that her son has been exhibiting fluctuations in his mood as well as verbal and physical aggression at home, at school, and in the community. Although Juan reports wanting to have a good relationship with his mother, he describes his interactions with her as stressful. Juan's father is not involved in his life. According to Juan's mother, Juan's father was physically abusive to both Juan and her. Juan's mother reports regretting that her son does not have a positive male role model in his life.

When asked for input regarding his treatment plan, Juan voices much frustration about his mother's tendency to be overly controlling. Juan reports wanting to obtain a driver's license, but he laments about his mother "not letting me drive." During the first session, Juan and his mother agree to the following treatment plan.

Treatment Plan

Name: Juan
Therapist: Michael Fulkerson, MAE, LPCC, CT/RTC
Strengths: Outspoken, extroverted, kind, and generous
Needs: Increased self-control and decision-making skills
Abilities: Athletic skills and intelligence
Preferences: Sports, music, and art
Barrier 1: Juan has a diagnosis of disruptive mood dysregulation disorder (DMDD). His targeted behaviors include an inability to control emotions as evidenced by verbal and physical aggression at home, at school, and in the community. Juan's lack of control and aggression has led to his mother to not permitting him to obtain his driver's license or permit.
Life Goal 1: "I want to learn to control my anger so that I can get my driver's license."

Treatment

Goal 1: "I will improve my ability to manage my anger by obtaining a driver's license."

Objective 1: Juan will journal what he is doing, thinking, and feeling and describe his physiological symptoms in at least four consecutive therapy sessions within the next sixty days.

Objective 2: Juan will explain to his therapist how his actions, thoughts, feelings, and physiology are similar to the functioning of a car within ninety days.

Objective 3: Juan will list at least three ways to manage his emotions more effectively within four months.

Objective 4: Juan will obtain his driver's permit within six months.

Interventions: Individual therapy for at least one hour per week. Therapist will introduce Juan to the basic concepts of choice theory and assist client in using reality therapy as a self-help method for the purpose of increasing Juan's ability to manage his emotions.

Barrier 2: Anxiety disorder, which includes negative self-talk, giving up easily, and frequent pacing. Juan scored 30 on the self-concept questionnaire. Scores below 60 are considered low.

Life Goal 2: "I would like to improve my self-esteem."

Treatment Goal 2: "I will show improved self-esteem as reflected in increasing my self-concept questionnaire score to at least 61.

Objective 1: Juan will identify three new relaxation skills and demonstrate these in the presence of his therapist within thirty days.

Objective 2: Juan will be able to list at least fifteen of his positive attributes within sixty days

Objective 3: Juan will identify at least five positive characteristics of the person he most admires within ninety days.

Objective 4: Juan will commit to at least three achievement plans to be more like the person he most admires within 120 days.

Objective 5: Juan will report achieving each of his three achievement plans to be more like the person he admires most within 150 days.

Interventions: Individual therapy will occur one time per week. Cognitive restructuring will be used to assist client in thinking differently about himself and his environment. Reframing will be used to assist in recognizing strengths, especially those that he perceives as weaknesses.

Barrier 3: Juan has a parent-child relational problem diagnosis. Juan and his mother report that their interactions usually involve arguing, blaming, and criticizing each other. Both Juan and his mother report feeling dissatisfied with their relationship.

Life Goal 3: Juan states, "I want to improve my relationship with my mother."

Treatment

Goal 3: Juan states, "Both me and my mother will agree that we have improved our relationship with each other."

Objective 1: Juan and his mother will come to an agreement regarding the rules and consequences to be followed at home within thirty days.

Objective 2: Both Juan and his mother will identify three positive results from replacing disconnecting relationship habits with connecting relationship habits within sixty days.

Interventions: Family therapy will occur two times per month. Parenting education will be provided to the guardian. Therapist will teach conflict-resolution skills to the family to strengthen family relationships.

Case 4: Chauncey (Age 4)

According to Chauncey's case manager and mother, Chauncey exhibits persistent defiance, impulsivity, and aggression (verbal and physical) on a daily basis. He is also destructive in the home environment and exhibits disregard for safety or any interventions by adults around him. He often requires physical restraint to maintain safety. Chauncey's mother is a single parent who reports feeling exhausted and overwhelmed with her child's behaviors. The mother admits to being inconsistent with her parenting methods.

Treatment Plan

Name: Chauncey
Therapist: Mike Fulkerson, LPCC, CT/RTC
Strengths: Active, strong-willed, independent, and inquisitive
Needs: Acceptance of limits
Abilities: Intelligent
Preferences: Playing with toys and less structured environments
Barriers: Chauncey's diagnoses include mood disorder, oppositional defiant disorder, and parent-child conflict. Physical aggression toward others and himself, including head-banging, biting, hitting, kicking, and AWOL risk. Multiple hospitalizations, including two within the past four months. Chauncey's mother reports that Chauncey shows a disregard for rules and is uncooperative with others. He is currently hospitalized with a transition to enter therapeutic foster care. The biological mother reports having little confidence to manage Chauncey's behavior and scored 15 on the Caring Habits Survey.
Life Goal 1: Chauncey states, "I want to have more privileges and stay out of the hospital."

Treatment

Goal 1: Chauncey says, "I want to maintain current placement for at least ninety consecutive days."
Objective 1: Chauncey will manage his emotions successfully having a thirty-day period free of safety-crisis management holds within the next three months.
Objective 2: While in the presence of his therapist, Chauncey will demonstrate at least three newly acquired skills for managing his emotions within the next thirty days.
Interventions: Individual therapy will occur twice monthly. Therapist will utilize play therapy and relaxation training to help Chauncey learn new ways to manage his emotions.
Life Goal 2: Chauncey states, "I want to live with my mother."

Treatment

Goal 2: Chauncey expressed that he wants to cooperate with rules so that "I will be reunified with my mother."

Objective 1: Chauncey will complete three task assignments given by therapist within twenty-one days.

Objective 2: Chauncey will have a successful "trial exit" from therapeutic foster care measured by no required intervention from on-call therapeutic foster care staff.

Interventions: Individual therapy will occur at least twice monthly. Reality therapy will be integrated with play therapy to assist Chauncey in learning to cooperate through the use of encouragement and setting limits.

Life Goal 3: Chauncey's mother states, "I want to better manage my son's behavior."

Treatment

Goal 3: Chauncey's mother expressed, "I will inform the therapist that I feel more confident and prepared to manage Chauncey's behavior when he returns home."

Objective 1: Chauncey's mother will improve her Caring Habits Survey score by at least ten points.

Objective 2: Chauncey's mother will describe to the therapist three things she is doing more effectively as a parent as a result of consultations with the therapist.

Interventions: Family therapy will occur at least two times per month. Choice theory/reality therapy parenting psychoeducation will be provided to assist the parent in relating to Chauncey in a less controlling, noncritical way through the use of William Glasser's seven caring habits.

As a self-directed/natural support intervention, Chauncey's mother will read one book on applying choice theory principles to her parenting.

Discharge Plan

Behavioral indicators that child/family is ready for discharge: Client will be reunified with his mother once he demonstrates stability of mood and behaviors as indicated by a period of ninety consecutive days without requiring hospitalization.

Goal for level of care/support for the child/family at discharge: To return to the biological family, home of his mother, and follow up with therapy, case management, and comprehensive community-support services.

Crisis Action Plan

Symptoms/behaviors that indicate a crisis: Defiance, verbal aggression, and physical aggression

Strategies to Manage Crises

1.  Provide empathic statements and encourage cooperation.
2.  Set firm limits and focus Chauncey on current behavior.
3.  Encourage Chauncey to self-evaluate his choices.
4.  Assist Chauncey in making a plan to do better.
5.  Allow natural consequences except in cases where safety is in question.
6.  Consult with on-call staff or therapist regarding treatment interventions.

Client 5: Jerry

Jerry is a fifty-six-year-old male who has been dealing with addiction to alcohol for many years. According to Jerry, his addiction to alcohol destroyed his career, his marriage, and his relationships with his children who no longer have contact with him. For the past several years, Jerry has been in and out of rehab treatment programs and homeless shelters. With the exception of living in a controlled setting, Jerry has been unable to maintain sobriety for more than a period of two or three months. He has just completed another twenty-eight-day inpatient program and is continuing treatment on an outpatient basis.

Treatment Plan

Name: Jerry
Therapist: Mike Fulkerson, LPCC, CT/RTC
Strengths: Personable, social skills, and intelligence
Needs: To remain sober when living outside a controlled setting (rehab, shelters, etc.)
Abilities: Excellent handyman skills and articulate in speech
Preferences: He identifies himself as having a preference for being around others. Jerry says he likes "making others happy."
Barriers: Jerry has a diagnosis of a substance use disorder. He has been unable to maintain independent living and remain sober for longer than two or three months outside a controlled setting.
Life Goal 1: Jerry states, "I want to get clean and sober so I can get my life back."

Treatment

Goal 1: Jerry expressed, "I will be able to achieve independent living and sobriety for at least one year."
Objective 1: Jerry will complete a cost-benefit analysis of three desired changes he wants to make in his life.
Objective 2: Jerry will identify the function(s) his substance use has been serving in terms of meeting his needs for love/belonging, power, freedom, and fun.
Objective 3: Jerry will develop a written strategy to replace his substance-using behaviors by listing alternative pathways to fulfill each of his unmet needs.
Objective 4: Jerry will develop a written relapse-prevention plan that will include a list of warning signs, effective coping skills, and a contact list of people who can help him.

Interventions: Individual therapy will occur one time per week. Therapist will provide Jerry with information regarding the use of choice theory and reality therapy as a self-help method in addition to other cognitive-behavioral techniques such as cognitive restructuring, guided imagery, and reframing.

A cost-benefit analysis will be used to assess Jerry's desire to change as well as his commitment level of maintaining sobriety.

As a self-directed intervention, Jerry will attend ninety AA meetings in ninety days to help him stay on the road to recovery.

# CHAPTER 7

---

# INTEGRATING CHOICE THEORY/ REALITY THERAPY WITH PERSON-CENTERED PLANNING

In recent years, person-centered care planning has moved to the forefront of the implementation of treatment and recovery planning in the behavioral health care system. Although there is solid research to support the person-centered care planning approach, Tondora, Miller, and Davidson (2012) have identified questions raised by practitioners regarding the limitations of the person-centered care-planning approach. The author's goals in this chapter are twofold. First, to provide a thorough description of how choice theory/reality therapy can be integrated with the principles of person-centered care planning. Second, to explain how the integration of choice theory/reality therapy treatment planning can address some of the concerns regarding a person-centered care-planning approach.

Setting Goals

As mentioned earlier, there are two types of goals to be familiar with when writing a treatment plan. First, the LIFE'S goal, which includes the acronym LIFE'S to represent the five basic needs, according to choice theory. This goal is stated using the client's own words, which are placed in quotations. The purpose of using the client's own words placed in quotations is to ensure that the treatment plan is a client-guided and client-driven plan.

Many practitioners have voiced concerns about clients giving input into the treatment plan. One of the concerns is that clients may not know what they want or will just give a vague statement as input. Another concern is that what the client wants may not be realistic, feasible, or positively stated or meet the criteria for medical necessity under insurance regulations for billing (Tondora, Miller, and Davidson 2012).

Reality therapists are able to go beyond these vague statements by accessing client quality world pictures and exploring what they really want, which is to have their five basic needs met. Please see the below discussion as an example of how a reality therapist may clarify what a client really wants.

Counselor: Please tell what you would like as your treatment plan goal.

Client: I want to control my anger.

Counselor: Why is it important for you to control your anger?

Client: So I can make some friends.

As one can see, the counselor was able to clarify that what the client really wants is more belonging in his/her life. By identifying what clients really want, more doors open, which can help people begin to see more options in fulfilling their needs, which increases psychological flexibility.

Next, let's take a look at a scenario in which a client expresses a goal that might not meet the medical necessity criteria for an insurance company to approve counseling services. Please look for how the counselor helps guide the client to defining a goal that may justify therapy.

Counselor: What goal would you like for your treatment plan?

Client: I want to take care of my case manager.

Counselor: Taking care of the case manager is important to you?

Client: Yes. I like helping other people.

Counselor: Helping other people can give us good feelings. What does it do for you when you help others?

Client: I feel like my life has meaning or purpose.

Counselor: So, what you really want is to have more meaning and purpose in your life.

In these examples, one can see how the counselors were able to assist the clients in relating their wants to needs. The goals are now more realistic, feasible, and accepting to a third-party payer source.

Another one of the aforementioned concerns was that some insurance companies want measurable treatment goals, especially with a time-limited service. In addition, since some therapists may not plan to keep a client on their caseload for twenty years, having a clear finish line for therapy will be important. This is where the service delivery/treatment goal comes into play. This type of goal answers two important questions: "How will you know when you have achieved your goal? How will we know when our therapeutic relationship is about to end?"

Another way to think about the service delivery/treatment goal is to see it as the operationalization of the life goal. Putting the life goal in measurable terms is a "language translation" that will resonate with insurance companies. Here is an example:

Client:      "My goal is to improve my self-esteem."

Counselor:   "Your score on the self-concept questionnaire reveals a low score, which is 30. Do you think a score of 30 reflects how your self-esteem is right now?"

Client:      "Yes."

Counselor:   "Do you believe this questionnaire would be a way of measuring progress with your self-esteem?"

Client:      "Yes."

Counselor:   "Within the next three to six months, what would you like for your self-concept score to be?"

Client:      "I would like to improve my self-concept survey score to above 60."

Counselor:   "So, you would like for your treatment goal to be that you will improve your self-esteem as reflected by increasing your self-concept survey to above 60."

Client:      "Yes."

Helping clients figure out goals can be a challenge. Sometimes people know exactly what they want and where to start, but at other times, it may be more of a struggle. Therefore, the basic needs-related questions may help them better decide what they want to work on right now in their lives.

## Love/Belonging

Who are the important people in your life right now? What do you like about them? What are you getting from these relationships that you do not want? What would you like to be getting from each of these important people in your life? Would you like to have more friends? Describe what you do to make friends. What will it take to increase your social network?

## Inner Control/Power/Achievement/Recognition

What is something you would like to achieve or accomplish? How important is faith/spirituality in your life? What are some things you can control that would help improve your self-worth? Would you like to work? What would you like to do? What would you like to improve about your work situation?

## Freedom/Independence/Autonomy

What would be something that would give you a sense of independence/ freedom? Describe some obstacles that prevent you from having more choices. Are you dealing with any legal issues right now? What rules do you live by? What do you have to do? What do you want to do? What do you not want to have to do or not want to do?

## Enjoyment/Fun/Learning

What are your interests or hobbies? What do you do for fun/enjoyment? What would you like to learn more about? What information do you want in order to get more pleasure/satisfaction out of life?

Survival/Self-Preservation/Health

What are your health concerns? How is your financial situation? How would you like to change your living situation, if at all?

Examples of LIFE'S Goals

Love/Belonging

- "I want a better relationship with my spouse/parent/sibling."
- "I want to have more friends."
- "I want to improve my social skills."

Inner Control/Power/Achievement

- "I want a GED."
- "I want to find a job."
- "I want to improve my self-confidence."

Freedom/Independence/Autonomy

- "I want to obtain independent living."
- "I want to buy a car."
- "I want to start my own business."

Enjoyment/Fun/Learning

- "I want to be able to entertain myself."
- "I want to learn something new."
- "I want to go on a vacation."

Survival/Self-Preservation/Health

- "I want to improve my health."
- "I want to achieve and maintain a healthy weight."
- "I want to exercise more."

Barriers

With traditional treatment planning, target behaviors and presenting problems were listed. The person-centered treatment-planning perspective uses the word "barriers" to replace issues, presenting problems, and target behaviors. One of the reasons for this change is to consider inclusion of external factors that may impact progress toward treatment goals. Barriers are things that stand in the way of goal attainment (Adams and Grieder 2014). One of the important questions to ask is this: "What are some obstacles that may keep the client from achieving his/her goals?" Listed below are some examples of barriers:

| | | |
|---|---|---|
| apathy/indifference | lack of insight | no transportation |
| conflicts in relationships | lack of self-awareness | pessimistic attitude |
| domestic violence | legal issues | physical disabilities |
| fighting | less effective self-talk | physical health diagnosis |
| grief/loss | limited community | poor impulse control |
| history of abuse | resources | poor work history |
| homelessness | limited income | speech impediment |
| indifference | low self-confidence | substance use |
| intellectual disabilities | low self-esteem | truancy |
| lack of clarity | mental health diagnosis | verbal aggression |
| lack of housing | no support system | |

As mentioned earlier, building upon strengths has been an essential part of reality therapy. As choice theory explains, it is easier for people to use organized behaviors than it is to create new behaviors through reorganization (Glasser 1998, Glasser 2011). Here are some examples of questions and statements to help access more effective organized behaviors:

- Tell me about a time when things were going well for you.
- What are some of the resources/people you can draw on to help you?
- What is something you are really proud of?
- Who do you prefer to spend time with?
- If your friends/family were here, what would they say that you do well?
- What do other people say they like about you?
- How do you spend your free time?
- What do you know a lot about?
- What are some things you would not change about yourself?
- Describe the times you are most at peace.
- What are your best qualities?
- What would you like to know about improving your health?

These kinds of questions and statements help the reality therapist become aware of talents, abilities, competencies, values, cultural influences, interests, resources, natural supports, attributes, and assets that can be incorporated into the treatment plan. Also, remember that many perceived weaknesses are strengths that have become maximized, so the technique of reframing can come in quite handy when working with clients/families who tend to focus on deficits rather than strengths.

Objectives

While treatment goals are related to the client's basic needs and quality world pictures, objectives are designed to address the behaviors necessary to obtain the goals, achieve quality world pictures, and satisfy basic needs. Objectives are incremental steps toward goal attainment/measure of progress, which describe how people will know they are making progress. Using action words, objectives describe the specific changes expected in measurable terms, including a target date for completion. Here are some examples of information-gathering questions/statements to assist in formulating objectives:

- What would it take to get what you want?
- How might you accomplish your goal?

- If the primary barrier were removed, what would you be doing differently?
- How will you know that you are making progress?
- What are some new thinking and acting skills you might be willing to use?
- What are some small steps you could take to move closer to your goal?
- What do other people need to see you doing to indicate that you are moving closer to your goal?
- What evidence could you provide that you are making progress toward your goal?

The information gathered from these questions/statements become the SMART (simple, measurable, attainable, relevant, and time-limited) objectives. Objectives are useful in helping people attend more to the process of change rather than outcome, which can help reduce the frustration that often leads to people feeling discouraged when their goals are not immediately achieved.

Another purpose of objectives is to address barriers that have prevented clients from achieving their goals. One way of formulating the objectives is to look at the steps that could be taken to overcome barriers. This is the rationale behind having multiple objectives for goals. Very seldom is there just one obstacle in the way of goal attainment (Adams and Grieder 2014).

Intervention

Interventions describe the services or treatments that will be provided in order to assist clients in obtaining their goals and objectives. In addition, interventions include who will be responsible for the service delivery or treatment as well as the intended purpose or impact as it relates to obtaining goals and objectives. The frequency and duration of services should also be specified (Adams and Grieder 2014). Examples of questions to gather input regarding interventions include:

- How do you see me helping you?
- What do you believe is the best treatment approach for you?

- What treatment strategies have been helpful in the past?
- What therapy methods have not been helpful?
- How can services best help you?
- Would you like to know more about all the services we have to offer?

The information gathered from these questions will provide the therapist with information needed to document what Adams and Grieder (2014) refer to as billable interventions. In addition to billable interventions, Adams and Grieder describe two types of non-billable interventions: self-directed and natural supports.

Self-directed interventions are designed to invite clients to take an active role in their own treatment (Adams and Grieder 2014). Such invitations are likely to promote self-determination while avoiding encouraging dependency. Self-directed actions go beyond just attending a service. Instead, they focus on how organized, effective behaviors and/or strengths will be incorporated into the treatment plan. Examples of questions to gather information about self-directed interventions include:

- What are some steps you can take to move closer to achieving your goals and objectives?
- What can you do to help yourself?
- Why is it important for you to do some things on your own?
- Which activities help you stay calm, relaxed, or focused?

As I was learning about self-directed interventions, I wondered how these differ from treatment objectives. After attending several trainings on person-centered recovery planning, I concluded that there are two major differences. Unlike treatment objectives, self-directed interventions do not need to be measurable—and they are not things that will necessarily be occurring during a therapy session or be carried out solely within the context of therapeutic services.

Adams and Grieder (2014) describe natural supporter interventions as interventions by unpaid people. These people may include family, friends, or volunteers. From a choice theory perspective, these interventions are of a primary importance because they are being implemented by the most important people in the client's life—and they will likely remain involved with the client long after therapeutic services have ended.

- How can the important people in your life help you?
- Who are some of the people in the community who can be of help to you?
- Where are some places you can go to find more natural supports?
- What can your support system do to assist you in achieving your goals and objectives?
- Describe some things natural supporters can avoid, which would not be helpful to you.

When documenting interventions, the counselor will want to identify specific aspects of therapy that would be used to assist the client and the rationale for the utilization of a particular technique (Adams and Grieder 2014). For instance, reality therapists may document that they are providing information regarding what Glasser (2000) refers to as the seven caring habits of relationships in order to enhance a client's social skills or ability to increase social connections.

Stephanie's Story (Background and Assessment Data)

Stephanie is a fifty-four-year-old Caucasian woman who grew up and currently lives in a small town in Kentucky. She is a deeply loving mother and grandmother. When her children were young, Stephanie relied heavily on her sister Rebecca to provide care and support when she was struggling with symptoms of bipolar disorder, PTSD (due to a history of childhood sexual abuse), and addiction. Most of her life, Stephanie and her children lived with Rebecca in the home that Rebecca owned. Her children are now thirty-two and thirty, married, and have children of their own. Previously, they visited Stephanie and Rebecca almost every weekend to enjoy big Sunday dinners together, but since Rebecca died nearly two years ago and Stephanie moved into her own small apartment, they rarely visit.

Since Rebecca's death, Stephanie has had trouble caring for herself. Over the past two years, she has started to use alcohol regularly, and symptoms of PTSD and bipolar disorder (e.g., nightmares, hypervigilance, sleep disturbance, fearfulness, and scattered thinking) have been very disruptive. She has been brought into the emergency room four times in the past three months due to severe intoxication. Emergency room personnel offered her medical detoxification and warned that her blood pressure was dangerously high. Stephanie was extremely frightened by these events, but she rejected their offer of a medical detoxification. On her last emergency room visit, the physician who evaluated her used civil law to put Stephanie on a medical detoxification unit at the hospital. This hospitalization is how the CMHC Behavioral Health Care Coordination program became involved with Stephanie.

Stephanie feels sad about her relationships with her children and grandchildren. Most of all, she wants to have a meaningful role in their lives. Her daughter, Candice, says that Stephanie was less of a mother to her and her brother than her Aunt Rebecca, but that she and her brother want to have her in their children's lives if Stephanie will take better care of herself. They do not visit her with their children because Stephanie's apartment is very small, dirty, and cluttered, and that makes the visits very uncomfortable for them.

Stephanie has been living in her own apartment for eighteen months, and for most of that time, she has been very overwhelmed by symptoms of mental illness and addiction. The loss of her sister, her greatest support, has left her feeling vulnerable and without a home. Stephanie has never lived alone and has not yet made this apartment a true home for herself. She gets very disorganized and overwhelmed when trying to clean the apartment, and it has been filling up with hundreds of books that Stephanie finds and brings home.

When Beverly died, the family sold the house and inherited the profits from the sale. Stephanie inherited $160,000. Candice sought support services for her mother when she discovered that Stephanie had been struggling, drinking, and spending large sums on lottery tickets. She also "loaned" thousands of dollars to people she had only recently met.

Stephanie's children are deeply saddened by their mother's illness. "She had been doing so well over the last ten years. I guess Aunt Rebecca's passing must have been very hard for her."

Stephanie has a number of strengths and interests that she can draw upon in order to overcome the difficulties she is currently experiencing.

Michael H. Fulkerson, LPCC-S

Stephanie is intelligent, well educated, and has worked successfully as a research assistant and writer. Her many interests include knitting, making baby clothes, walking, and reading. Stephanie has enjoyed long periods of time when she was feeling well and only rarely had problems caused by symptoms or alcohol. During these times, Stephanie has actively used both professional supports as well as a range of personal wellness strategies.

Summary of Assessed Needs

Stephanie has quality world pictures in multiple need areas that could be addressed in future treatment plans. The quality world pictures that are most relevant at the present time to her overall goal of spending more time with her children and grandchildren are:

- Family relationships: Stephanie's children, Candice and William, do not want to visit their mother when she is drinking alcohol because she can be short and irritable, especially when she stops taking care of herself and her apartment. They complain that the space is so filthy that it is not safe for the grandchildren to be there. Candice and William say they would be willing to visit if Stephanie could take better care of herself and her apartment.
- Symptom management: Stephanie has survived highly traumatic events in her life. She was sexually molested from the age of nine to thirteen by a trusted adult male neighbor, after which she increasingly developed symptoms of PTSD, including flashbacks, sleep disturbance, depression, and hypervigilance toward others. She has had periods of time when she used effective coping strategies, managed her symptoms, and felt she was doing well. For the past two years, Stephanie's symptoms of irritability and severe depression have become much worse, and she tends to resort to the use of alcohol to manage her distress.
- Health concerns: Stephanie has high blood pressure that recently has been uncontrolled. Rebecca played a big role in helping Stephanie with doctors' appointments and medications, but since Rebecca died, Stephanie has not been taking medication for hypertension or visiting her doctor. At the same time, while Stephanie is terrified of having a

heart attack or stroke, she is even more frightened of meeting with doctors since her trauma history makes her intensely fearful of adult men in closed environments.

- Social relationships: Stephanie acknowledges that since Rebecca died, she has not visited with other family or friends. She has belonged to a book club but says now that she cannot concentrate on reading because it tires her eyes. She says, "I guess I am lonely, and that can get me into trouble." (This means she often uses alcohol when she feels lonely).

- Residential support: Stephanie reports that she has "never been much of a housekeeper." Rebecca performed all of the household chores. Stephanie feels overwhelmed by the amount of cleaning and laundry she has to do. She does not know where to start, and at times, she reports feeling too depressed to initiate any of these activities.

Stephanie's Treatment Plan

Individual/Family Strengths

Intelligent, well-educated, worked successfully, past success using coping skills for an extended period of time, knitting, making baby clothes, and walking.

Barriers

Bipolar disorder and PTSD symptoms, becomes intoxicated when lonely, very disorganized, struggles with housekeeping, little contact with her family, overspending, and a dependent relationship with her sister who died two years ago.

Goal 1

Stephanie's life goal: "I want to improve my relationship with my children and grandchildren."

Her service-delivery/treatment goal is based on self-reporting: Stephanie will report having a satisfactory relationship with her children and grandchildren.

## Objectives

1. Within twenty-eight days, Stephanie will clean one room in her house, based on self-report.
2. Within sixty days, Stephanie will list five new ways she can put more love/belonging in her life to combat feelings of loneliness.
3. Within ninety days, Stephanie will describe to her therapist at least seven behaviors she has used to improve her relationships with her children and grandchildren.

## Interventions

1. Individual therapy will occur weekly to assist Stephanie with addressing issues related to past trauma. Aspects of choice theory/reality therapy will be used to provide Stephanie with information about how to improve her relationship habits with others as well as herself.
2. Case-management services will be provided monthly. The case manager will provide information about local support groups and link Stephanie to services, which may lead to more social support.
3. Community-support services will occur weekly for a duration of six months. The community-support associate will provide opportunities for Stephanie to practice new relationship habits in a community setting.
4. Stephanie's self-directed intervention will be that she will join a support group within the next three months to increase her level of involvement with other people.

Goal 2

Stephanie's second life goal: "I want to get my blood pressure under control."

Her second service-delivery goal is that Stephanie will maintain a blood pressure reading of no higher than 140/90 for thirty consecutive days.

## Objectives

1. Within the next thirty days, Stephanie will complete a cost-benefit analysis of taking or not taking her hypertensive medications.
2. Within the next sixty days, Stephanie will identify four changes she could make that could have a positive impact on her health.
3. Within the next ninety days, Stephanie will memorize five elements of an effective action plan.

## Interventions

1. Individual therapy will occur weekly. Choice theory/reality therapy will be utilized to assess Stephanie's level of commitment to change, prioritize her values, promote self-evaluation, and develop effective action plans to improve her health.
2. The primary physician will monitor and prescribe medications to help regulate Stephanie's blood pressure. Appointments will occur at least every six months.
3. Stephanie's self-directed invention will be that she will monitor and log her blood pressure daily.
4. Stephanie's natural supports will initiate contact with Stephanie on a monthly basis to provide support and help encourage progress.

# CHAPTER 8

## CASE CONCEPTUALIZATION EXAMPLE

Once upon a time, one of the major criticisms of reality therapy was that it lacked a solid theory to support it. In present time, reality therapy has one of the most thorough and comprehensive theories to support it. Choice theory is the justification for reality therapy. Each component of reality therapy is supported by choice theory, the theoretical lens that reality therapists use to conceptualize clients. A prior case conceptualization is essential to writing an effective treatment plan.

In this chapter, using an outline developed by Robert Wubbolding, the author illustrates how a case can be conceptualized through the lens of choice theory. In addition, a treatment plan example is added to show how the case conceptualization is the foundation for the treatment plan. In this case description, the author describes how a reality therapist can use choice theory/reality therapy to "flush out" PTSD symptoms.

Case Description

Name: Ben
Gender: Male
Age: 10
Race/Ethnicity: Caucasian

Ben currently lives with his aunt who has custody over him as well as his two siblings. Both biological parents are incarcerated due to abuse, neglect, and illegal substance use. His trauma history includes physical abuse, exposure to domestic violence, parents arrested due to drug involvement, growing up in a drug-saturated environment, and custody removed from the parents.

His current legal guardian has been charged with physical abuse and has been court-ordered to avoid using physical discipline. Ben mentions that his aunt says, "What happens here, stays here!" He says that he has to be careful when speaking with behavioral health professionals.

Allegations of abuse by the aunt have been referred to social services, but recent social services investigations have been finding the allegations "unsubstantiated" and imply the behavioral health professionals making the reports are being "manipulated" by Ben. In addition, the legal guardian has declined any participation in therapy and has stated, "Ben is the problem. He is the one who needs to be fixed by therapy."

Case Conceptualization

Throughout the first decade of life, Ben has struggled to meet his need for love/belonging due to the dysfunction with his family of origin. He has severely lacked having effective role models for good mental health as evidenced by the legal issues of his biological parents, which have contributed to the instability in Ben's relationships with them.

Thus far, Ben has learned to play the role of "the scapegoat" by assuming responsibility for the dysfunction in his family because his adult relatives have been unable to accept responsibility for their own behaviors. The primary reason for the need for therapy is to invite Ben to recognize that although he is responsible for his actions, he is not responsible for the actions of his family members. The hope is with counseling, Ben will gain more freedom by being able to remove some of his self-blame, which will make it easier for him to have more self-determination.

## Diagnostic Characteristics

Ben has been referred to therapy due to exhibiting poor impulse control at home, in school, and in the community. He has exhibited verbal and physical aggression in all three settings. Frequently, he is described as argumentative, disrespectful, inattentive, and possessing poor judgment. His current diagnoses include impulse control disorder and PTSD. Ben reports a significant amount of trauma related to the past abuse by his parents. Reported symptoms include recurrent nightmares, feelings of hopelessness, irritability, difficulty concentrating, and intense feelings of guilt. On the Child Post-traumatic Stress Scale, Ben score a 41, which is an extremely high score.

## Current Need Satisfaction

One of Ben's strongest attributes is his ability to articulate. His verbal acumen and insight are well above average for his age. As a result, he has been able to identify feelings such as guilt, hopelessness, and paranoia. Accompanying these feelings, he has reported less effective self-talk statements such as: "It is all my fault," "I am a snitch," "I must not make a mistake," "No one will listen to me," and "I can't do better."

Ben is also aware of headaches and stomachaches that are often associated with these unwanted thoughts and feelings. A sense of peace is a feeling that he has verbalized wanting to have more often. However, Ben seemed to have limited information as how to create more of a sense of peace in his life. Throughout the sessions with Ben, the therapist understood that he appeared to have high-intensity needs for love/belonging, power/achievement, and freedom/independence, which have gone largely unfulfilled throughout his first decade of life. The therapist recognized that Ben had above average ability to see humor. This ability has been a primary pathway to fulfill his need for fun/enjoyment.

Perceived Internal/External Locus of Control

Less effective self-talk statements, such as "It is all my fault that my parents went to jail," indicate that Ben tends to view his responsibility in his parental relationships from a high level of perception. Also, his statements like "I can't do any better" indicates more of an external locus of control because he sees success as being beyond his capabilities. His perception may have been influenced by receiving parental messages such as "You cannot do any better," which have been subtle ways of contributing to his lack of self-worth and autonomy.

Examples of Sustain Talk and Change Talk

After Ben stated that he was to blame for his parents losing custody of him and his siblings, the therapist asked if this belief was helpful to him. His response of "yes" is an example of sustain talk and indicated to the therapist that Ben was in the earlier stages of change (pre-contemplative or contemplative), which would likely lead to less of a commitment to change. Therefore, more relationship building and negotiating a helping role may be necessary to assist Ben in evaluating his commitment to change.

In another instance, Ben demonstrated "change" talk when he identified wanting to have more of a sense of peace in his life, feeling better about himself, and better relationships with those around him. Overall, Ben appears to be in the contemplative stage of change, which means it may be a challenge to elicit more than an "I'll try" level of commitment.

Quality World Exploration

Three techniques were employed by the therapist to access Ben's quality world. First is the use of exploratory statements, such as, "Describe your picture of being happy. Tell me about the important people in your life." Although these types of statements obtain much of the same information that could be gathered with a question, exploratory statements have some advantages over the use of a question. Exploratory statements can access a broader range of information in what might seem to be a less threatening manner as perceived by the client, especially clients in the pre-contemplative and contemplative stages of change.

Second, after acquiring general information via the use of exploratory statements, the therapist followed up with specific questions to gain information regarding which quality world pictures are being satisfied and which ones are not. Examples of these questions include:

- What do you like about each of the important people in your life?
- What are you getting that you do not want?
- What would you like to be getting?

Third, when asked about his goals, Ben often spoke more about his problems. To help shift the session in a more productive direction, the therapist would often reframe the problems into solutions. For example, Ben might say, "I don't want any more hassles in my relationships." The therapist would paraphrase this statement by saying something like, "You want to have more peace in your relationships."

Organized Behaviors

Some of Ben's strengths include that he performs well academically. His grades are above average. He also enjoys music and sports. Ben reports feelings of boredom as seldom being a problem. Unlike many of his peers, he has discovered ways to put fun in his life without getting into trouble.

His abilities include being able to articulate his feelings at a level beyond his developmental age. Ben's ability to express himself both verbally and written helps enhance his ability to benefit from counseling. Due to previous therapeutic interventions, Ben was already familiar with relaxation techniques like breathing exercises, guided imagery, and meditation.

Although Ben seems to have adequate social skills and can relate well to others, he reports preferring to speak about personal issues in one-to-one conversations as opposed to group situations. Also, he tends to reveal more about his perceived world when he is not in the presence of his family. Ben states that he prefers individual therapy to group or family therapy.

Reorganized Behaviors

Some of the areas that may require reorganizing may be helping Ben think differently about himself and his relationships with family members. Ben's sense of inner control may be enhanced if he is able to recognize some of the choices he is making as well as some of the options that are available to him. By seeing himself as part of the solution, he could feel more encouraged rather than feeling discouraged when he sees himself as the "problem child" in his family.

How the Counselor Established a Safe, Trusting Counseling Environment

Some of the key components to establishing a safe, trusting counseling environment include empathic listening, suspending judgment, and the use of humor. The reality therapist used reflections, empathy, and acceptance to establish a connection with Ben. Also, props and a therapeutic game were used to help incorporate humor into the sessions.

Therapeutic Alliance

The reality therapist sees the client as "the expert" of the content in his/her own quality world. Therefore, it is essential that the reality therapist use the client's quality world pictures as the central guidance mechanism in the development of treatment goals and objectives. This person-centered approach to treatment planning is supported by much research that shows clients are more responsive to treatment when respect is given to their input and included in the treatment plan.

Using Choice Theory/Reality Therapy as a Method of Person-Centered Planning

Now that a thorough case conceptualization has been completed, the clinician can implement reality therapy into the treatment-planning process. This process will begin with taking a look at how to define barriers, goals, objectives, and interventions.

Life Goal 1: Ben states, "I want to have more peace in my life and less stress."

Barriers

Some major barriers have been identified. First, Ben scored a 41 on the Child Post-traumatic Stress Scale (CPSS). This score indicates an extremely high level of stress. According to Ben, the score on the CPSS accurately measures his present level of stress, and he acknowledged that the CPSS would likely be an accurate way to measure his progress. Second, Ben exhibits a high degree of less effective self-talk statements. And finally, his biological family may not be supportive of Ben being open and honest about what he is thinking or feeling when speaking with behavioral health team members.

Both Ben and his caregiver have reported that Ben has high levels of anxiety, which have contributed to disruptive behaviors in the classroom and at home. Poor grades and an inability to maintain friendships have been well-documented. These barriers are often accompanied by less effective self-talk statements, such as "It is all my fault" or "I am a bad kid."

Individual/Family Strengths

Ben is quite insightful and articulate for his age. He is fairly easy to engage in therapeutic activities and discussions. His family allows Ben to participate in therapy despite possible mistrust of behavioral health professionals.

Service Delivery/Treatment Goal 1: Ben will increase his ability to manage PTSD symptoms as evidenced by improving his CPSS score of 41 to below 20.

Objective 1: Ben will list three less effective self-talk statements that negatively impact his friendships and academic performance within thirty days.

Objective 2: Ben will list three more effective self-talk statements that positively impact his friendships and academic performance within thirty days.

Objective 3: Within forty-five days, Ben will document three things that are really important for him to accomplish.

Objective 4: Ben will memorize at least five elements of an effective plan within sixty days.

Objective 5: In sessions with his therapist, Ben will describe three successes he has accomplished with regard to following through with achievement plans within ninety days.

Objective 6: Ben will share with his therapist that he has followed through with three successful, self-initiated achievement plans within ninety days.

Interventions

1. Sessions with individual therapist will occur weekly for a duration of thirteen weeks. Choice theory/reality therapy will be used to assist Ben in cognitively restructuring his thinking and improving his relationship with himself. Aspects of narrative therapy will be integrated with reality therapy to assist Ben in increasing awareness of his behavior and improving his ability to stabilize his emotions.

2. Case manager will maintain at least monthly contact with Ben and his guardian. Case-management services will focus on linking Ben with community activities that will likely increase his social network and strengthen his social skills.

3. As a self-directed intervention, Ben will participate in at least one extracurricular school activity to practice new social skills.

4. Community support services will occur weekly. The community-support associate will act as an extension of the therapy in the community by teaching coping skills and social skills so that Ben can increase his natural supports and improve his relationship with himself.

# CHAPTER 9

## KEY ASPECTS OF CHOICE THEORY/REALITY THERAPY FOR THE CASE OF BEN

In the previous chapter, an example of how a case can be conceptualized from a choice theory lens was documented. In addition, a treatment plan was constructed describing how reality therapy will be utilized for the duration of treatment. Using the same case of Ben, the author will describe how key aspects of choice theory/reality therapy were utilized.

Focusing on Current Behavior

With Ben being quite articulate for his age in identifying feelings, the reality therapist focused on his total behaviors. Since the feeling component is the dimension that people are most likely to be aware of in a given moment, the reality therapist asked Ben to compile a list of "unwanted" and "wanted" feelings that Ben has been experiencing. He identified guilt, hopelessness, fear, and paranoia as some of the most troubling feelings. According to Ben, he has been dealing with unwanted feelings twenty-four hours a day, seven days per week. When asked to identify positive feelings, Ben identified having a sense of peace as one of the most important feelings he would like to have more often.

After compiling the two lists, the reality therapist asked Ben if he noticed anything different about the two lists. Ben recognized that the unwanted feelings list was substantially longer. The reality therapist pointed out to Ben that this illustrates how we are more aware of unwanted feelings than wanted feelings because when we have what we want, the motivation to obtain it diminishes. One of the teaching points at that moment was to emphasize how we are more aware of when our needs are *not* met than when they are. The reality therapist added that this potential lack of awareness is why it is so important to remember to take time to count our blessings rather than focusing so much on our afflictions.

One of the ways in which a reality therapist works differently from other therapists is to avoid discussing the feelings in isolation from the other components of the total behavior (Wubbolding 2011). While providing counseling to Ben, the reality therapist connected Ben's reported unwanted feelings with his less effective self-talk statements. The procedure of self-evaluation was implemented by asking Ben to list thoughts that have been either untrue or not helpful. Additionally, the unhelpful thoughts were defined as "stinkin' thinkin'."

Ben identified the following thoughts as "stinkin' thinkin' thoughts" that are untrue and/or not helpful:

- It is all my fault.
- I am a snitch.
- I must not make a mistake.
- No one will listen to me.
- I can't do better.

The therapist asked Ben to write these thoughts on bathroom tissue paper and tape each of the statements on to a dry erase board.

The reality therapist incorporated some teaching of choice theory by explaining how total behaviors included four inseparable components: activity, thinking, feeling, and physiology. Emphasis was placed on changing the thinking and acting components, which are the most controllable. Next, the reality therapist used a story to teach the concept of "reverse paranoia," which is defined by Wubbolding (2004) as approaching someone as a potential ally as opposed to an adversary. This story was used to illustrate how one's perception is accompanied by other total behaviors.

Ben spontaneously wrote two broad categories on the dry erase broad: his allies and his enemies. For his ally category, Ben listed the name of his therapist and case manager. He listed a plethora of other names as his enemies (teachers, peers, etc.) and placed his aunt in the neutral category. When asked if he would to like to have more allies, Ben acknowledged that this would be nice.

The reality therapist challenged Ben to convert his "stinkin'" thoughts into more "pleasant odor" thoughts. When Ben really appeared to struggle with this challenge, the reality therapist provided much needed assistance in this area by helping Ben with the "I am a snitch ... It is all my fault" less effective self-talk by stating it was not his fault that he told others what his parents were doing because Ben was acting to protect himself and his siblings as well as ensuring that his parents get the help that they needed.

Ben commented that the reality therapist was the only one besides his case manager who had ever told him that he was not to blame for his parents losing parental custody and being in jail. According to Ben, his family blamed him completely. The session drew to a close with Ben changing his less effective self-talk statements to more effective self-talk statements. The session concluded with a ceremonial "flushing of the stinkin' thinkin'," which was a humorous way to end the session by Ben flushing the bathroom tissue paper of "stinkin'" thoughts down the toilet.

Integration of a Narrative Therapy Technique

The reality therapist asked Ben, "If we were going to make a movie about your life, describe the script. What would the title be? Who would be cast in the starring roles?"

Once Ben selected his cast members, the reality therapist recommended including the following things: the "best things in my life" and the "worst things in my life."

Ben had little difficulty writing the narrative, but he did appear to have a high level of anxiety when asked if he would care to share it with someone. Ben disclosed that he did not mind sharing it with the reality therapist, but he would prefer not to read it aloud himself.

With Ben's permission, the reality therapist read some of the narrative aloud to Ben in the session. Throughout the narrative, it was quite apparent how Ben had been impacted by living in a drug-saturated environment filled with shame-bound beliefs. He wrote about liking the smell of marijuana and associating it with his parents. He also wrote about avoiding his mother when she smelled like beer, cigarettes, and "very bad weed" because of being afraid that she might be abusive.

One of the things that really surprised the therapist was when he wrote, "She (Mother) was so high it really scared us, but no matter what, we love her, we will always love her, and we still love her no matter what my therapist says."

After reading this last line, the reality therapist looked up and could not see Ben because he was hiding under the table. Ben told the reality therapist that he thought his therapist would be so angry when the last line of the narrative was read. The reality therapist informed Ben that he was not angry with him and explained that he was pleased that Ben trusted him enough to be so honest.

## Use of Self-Evaluation

The reality therapist invited Ben to explore two self-evaluation questions:

- Is it true that you are completely responsible for your parents being in jail and for you and your siblings being in foster care?
- Does it help you to take responsibility for the actions of your family members?

Both questions were asked in a curious and nonjudgmental tone. While responding to these questions, Ben shared with the therapist that he believed that his family was correct when they told him it was all his fault that his parents were incarcerated—and that Ben was no longer in their custody. He also stated that it benefits him to assume all of the blame because it is easier to get along with his family when he accepts all of the responsibility.

Rather than continue to challenge Ben's perception, the reality therapist decided to accept that Ben's belief was serving a purpose for him and expressed empathy. The reality therapist said, "Your acceptance of all the blame makes sense. You have learned that it is easier to live with your family members and be around them because you are the one who is strong enough to assume the responsibility for the circumstances of your family. Maybe you are right. For now, perhaps the best thing is for you to accept all responsibility even though you know deep down inside that other family members have responsibilities that they are not ready to accept. Someday you may want to let go all of this responsibility—and then you can get rid of it."

Ben smiled and stated, "Then I can just flush it down the toilet!"

The reality therapist responded, "Yes, you can flush it all down the toilet. But, for now, maybe you just need to stay 'on the pot' a little longer before you're ready to flush." At that moment, the reality therapist realized that the "stinkin' thinkin'" activity has made a lasting impact with Ben. This lasting impact was likely due to the activity incorporating a multisensory approach.

One of the myths about reality therapy is that feelings are not addressed. Although reality therapy places emphasis on actions, Wubbolding (2017) states, "This emphasis does not diminish the necessity of exploring clients' self-talk about their thoughts and what their gut feelings are about the current situation."

As documented above, a reality therapist can be quite empathic while using reflective statements, which can involve paraphrasing using the language of choice theory. Through the use of effective paraphrasing, the reality therapist can translate external control language to the language of choice theory. The result is that those receiving help will be encouraged to see more choices and have more hope. Because Ben can now recognize and appreciate his choices, he is now in more effective control of his life.

The final session concluded with the reality therapist readministering the CPSS as a post-response measure. Ben scored a 19 on the CPSS post-response measure. Although his score was still considered a high enough score to warrant a diagnosis of PTSD, it is surely indicative of progress as evidenced by Ben's pre-response measure CPSS score of 41.

# CHAPTER 10

# CONCLUSION

In this final chapter, I would like to summarize the book, add some concluding thoughts, and provide some tips for integrating choice theory/reality therapy with person-centered planning.

In chapter 1, I was able to explain my purpose for writing the book, describe how treatment planning with choice theory and reality therapy is different from traditional treatment planning, and compare choice theory/reality therapy to other psychotherapy treatment planning models.

Chapter 2 was divided into two parts: choice theory case conceptualization and reality therapy treatment planning. This chapter described how choice theory can serve as a solid theory for developing a case conceptualization. Also, I described how reality therapy can be used to develop and execute a treatment plan.

Chapter 3 and chapter 6 did not contain that much new information in this edition, but the content and case examples were updated to be more consistent with person-centered planning.

Chapter 5 provided a nice framework for completing progress notes using the GDIP model. New information was added regarding the documentation of facts and relevant treatment information.

Chapter 7 described how choice theory/reality therapy can be integrated with person-centered planning. The information in this chapter shows just how compatible choice theory/reality therapy is with person-centered planning principles. In addition, choice theory/reality therapy is described as being capable of addressing some of the limitations and criticisms of person-centered planning.

Chapter 8 included a thorough description of a case conceptualization from a choice theory perspective, and chapter 9 provided a case study description of reality therapy procedure implementation based on the choice theory case conceptualization. My goal was to show how well choice theory justifies each reality therapy procedure implemented in the case study.

My hope is that this book will be a valuable resource for clinicians looking to integrate choice theory/reality therapy into their clinical practices. I also hope this book will serve as a primer for any beginning clinician who is looking to provide interventions based on a sound treatment plan.

Integrating Choice Theory/Reality Therapy with Person-Centered Planning

Choice theory/reality therapy has much in common with person-centered planning. Both have the goal of fostering intrinsic motivation, seeking input from the client, and encouraging self-determination. The author has several recommendations for integrating choice theory/reality therapy with person-centered care planning.

First, using "person-first" language throughout the treatment plan, including using the person's first name throughout the document. Using language such as "a person diagnosed with schizophrenia" rather than "a schizophrenic" helps minimize the effects of labeling. Remember that from a choice theory perspective, diagnoses describe organized total behaviors rather than defining the person or explaining his/her behavior.

Second, treatment outcomes measures (goals and objectives) written in positive terms. For example, instead of "I just want to be less depressed," consider "I want to feel good enough to keep and maintain a job." Like Adlerian therapy (Carlson & Englar-Carlson 2013), choice theory teaches that all behavior has a purpose. Glasser (1998) extends the concept by stating that all behavior has a purpose for fulfilling needs and satisfying quality pictures. Treatment outcomes on the plan are about finding and maintaining meaning and purpose in one's life and not just symptom reduction or compliance.

Third, incorporating strengths into the goals, objectives, and interventions of the treatment plan. Treatment planning happens more smoothly when we assist people by using effective organized behaviors as opposed to creating new reorganized behaviors.

Fourth, listing barriers that are relevant in interfering with treatment outcomes. Barriers include going beyond client diagnoses to describe the client's unique perceived experience of symptoms and distress. Barriers could be external factors, such as legal restrictions, environment, or location. Many internal factors related to total behaviors or perception could also be viewed as barriers, such as an external locus of control or ambiguous quality world pictures.

Fifth, writing quality treatment objectives. In addition to the SMART criteria, there are other important characteristics. Objectives need to be comprehensible to the person served, have meaning/purpose, and be concrete enough to know definitively (yes/no) if it was achieved or not by the end of the review period. Another characteristic would be individualizing the objectives of the plan rather than all objectives defaulting to a standard update cycle, such as every sixty days. Finally, the objectives need to go beyond service participation and focus on the desired behavior change associated with a specific intervention.

Sixth, professional interventions describe who is providing the service, identify the billable service, determine the service frequency and duration, and provide the purpose and intent of the intervention. Of course, describing the rationale for using specific interventions will be easier for the therapist who uses a theory-driven approach.

# APPENDIX

Expectations of TCS/Intensive In-Home Services

## What We Will Do for You

1. Help you identify your goals for the program.
2. Help you determine what is effective and ineffective in reaching these goals.
3. Give information regarding alternative strategies to reach your goals.
4. Suspend judgment regarding your past efforts to achieve your goals.
5. Maintain confidentiality with the exception of the information that is necessary to ensure someone's safety.
6. Provide a need-fulfilling atmosphere to encourage family enrichment.

## What We Will Not Do for You

1. Tell you how to be a parent or how to live your life.
2. Give you a quick-fix solution. Things often get worse before getting better.
3. Take credit for your successes or failures.
4. Be expected to be providers or receivers of food, rewards, transportation, or money.
5. Be a babysitter or part of a companionship program.

6. Have our services used as a reward or punishment.
7. Communicate through email, texting, or social media.

## What You Will Be Expected to Do

1. Keep appointments and be punctual. Two unexcused absences could result in your child being returned to a waiting list for services.
2. Dedicate as many as three hours per week* to our sessions.
3. Work hard.
4. Remain focused on family treatment goals and objectives.

## What You Will Not Be Expected to Do

1. Make a long-term commitment to our program.
2. Tolerate our staff not honoring their commitments.
3. Provide staff with gifts, money, gift cards, etc. (Accepting gifts is a violation of agency policy and professional ethical codes.)

*Intensive in-home services only

Your signature below indicates that you understand and are in agreement with the expectations listed above.

(Signature) Date (Witness) Date

# Basic Needs Assessment for Child/Youth

Baseline date:
Mid-treatment date:
Closure date:

---

Please use a 0–10 scale (with 0 being the lowest and 10 being the highest) to answer the questions.

1. How physically healthy are you?
2. How well do you get along with the important people in your life?
3. How well do you like yourself?
4. How much control do you feel you have over your life?
5. How much fun/enjoyment are you having in your life?

Name of child:
Staff:

# Basic Needs Assessment by Parent(s) of Child/Youth

Baseline date:
Mid-treatment date:
Closure date:

---

Please use the following 0–10 (with 0 being the lowest and 10 being the highest) scale to answer the following questions:

1. How physically healthy is your child?
2. How well does your child get along with others?
3. Rate your child's self-esteem.
4. How much self-control does your child possess?
5. How much does your child seem to enjoy life?

Name of child:
Staff:

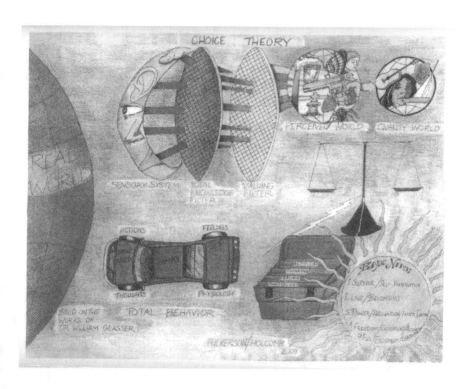

THE REALITY THERAPY SANDWICH

SELF-EVALUATION

ACTION PLANNING (SPECIFIC, SIMPLE, IMMEDIATE, INDEPENDENT, & START PLAN)

ASSESSING LOCUS OF CONTROL

EXPLORING CURRENT BEHAVIORS (ACTIONS, THOUGHTS, FEELINGS & PHYSIOLOGY)

OBTAINING A COMMITMENT

EXPLORING QUALITY WORLD PICTURES

RELATIONSHIPS
SEVEN CARING HABITS:
1.SUPPORTING        5.TRUSTING
2.ENCOURAGING   6.RESPECTING
3.LISTENING          7.NEGOTIATING
4.ACCEPTING

ADAPTED FROM THE WORKS OF DR WILLIAM GLASSER

FULKERSON/HOLCOMB 2008

# ABOUT THE AUTHOR

Michael Fulkerson is a licensed professional clinical counselor employed at RiverValley Behavioral Health in Owensboro, Kentucky. He serves as the program manager of Therapeutic Community Support Services. Mr. Fulkerson is also a senior faculty member of William Glasser International. His past work experiences have included inpatient therapy, domestic violence and substance abuse counseling, therapeutic foster care, and adjunct faculty status at Lindsey Wilson College.

# GLOSSARY OF KEY TERMS

caring habits. Relationship behaviors that move people closer together. When properly implemented into therapy, an environment conductive to the establishment of a therapeutic alliance is established.

choice theory. An internal control psychology that views human behavior as being driven by five basic needs: love/belonging, inner control/power/achievement, freedom/independence/autonomy, enjoyment/fun, and survival/self-preservation/health. A theory to conceptualize human behavior, it serves as the justification for reality therapy.

cognitive restructuring. A technique used in counseling that encourages clients to think differently about their problems. The purpose is to help clients have more effective thinking behaviors by changing what they do.

Cost-benefit analysis. A cognitive-behavioral technique involving evaluating the advantages and disadvantages of specific attitude or belief.

perceived world. A collection of images, including the positive, negative, and neutral ones. It is also known as the "all we know world."

perception. The information received from the external world, resulting from behavioral choices and composed of the perceived world and perceptual filters.

perception filters. Lenses through which human beings see the world and place values on the information received from it.

person-centered planning. A process for coordinating services and treatment interventions in a way that is driven and directed by the individual receiving the services.

Pete's Pathogram. Arlin V. Peterson created a needs assessment designed to provide a graphic illustration of an individual's perceived need intensity, time invested, and success in fulfilling the five basic needs according to choice theory.

quality world. A world that human beings create in their heads that is a reflection of how they want their perceived worlds to appear. It is composed of desires and images that possess quality. There are hundreds or thousands of mental pictures. These pictures are the pathways through which basic needs are satisfied.

reality therapy. Created by William Glasser, this method of helping people is comprised of environmental components and procedures that lead to change. It serves as an invitation for people to accept responsibility for their actions and find more effective ways of getting their needs satisfied.

total behavior. A description of human behavior as being comprised of four components: acting, thinking, feeling, and physiology. These four behavior components are inseparable and serve a purpose.

WDEP: An acronym used to help remember the procedures of reality therapy. Each letter represents questions and ideas related to the practice of reality therapy (wants, doing, evaluation, and planning).

# BIBLIOGRAPHY

Adams, N., & Grieder. D. (2014). *Treatment Planning for Person-Centered Care:*
*Shared Decision-Making for Whole Health* (2ⁿᵈ ed.). San Diego, CA: Elsevier Academic Press.

Carlson, J. D., & Englar-Carson, M. (2013). "Alderian therapy." In J. Frew & M. D.

Spiegler (Eds.), *Contemporary Psychotherapies for a Diverse World* (87–130). New York, NY: Routledge Taylor & Francis Group.

Corey, G. (2017). *Theory and Practice of Psychotherapy (10ᵗʰ ed.).* Boston, MA: Cengage Learning.

Glasser, W. (1965). *Reality Therapy.* New York, NY: Harper Row.

Glasser, W. (1990). *The Quality School.* New York, NY: HarperCollins.

Glasser, W. (1994). *Choice Theory Manager.* New York, NY: Harper Perennial, 1994.

Glasser, W. (2003). *Warning: Psychiatry Can Be Hazardous to Your Mental Health.*
New York, NY: HarperCollins.

Glasser, W. (1994). *The Choice Theory Manager.* New York: Harper Perennial.

Glasser, W. (1998). *Choice Theory.* New York, NY: Harper Collins.

Glasser, W. (2005). *Defining Mental Health as a Public Health Issue.* Chatsworth, CA: The William Glasser Institute.

Glasser, W. (2011). *Take Charge of Your Life.* Bloomington, IN: iUniverse.

Glasser, W., and Glasser, C. (2000). *Getting Together and Staying Together.* New York, NY: Harper Collins.

Jacobs, E. (1994). *Impact Therapy.* Lutz, FL: Psychological Assessment Resources, Inc.

Mitchell, C. (2009). *Effective Techniques for Dealing with Highly Resistant Clients (2ⁿᵈ. ed.).* Johnson City, TN: Clifton W. Mitchell, Publisher.

Peterson, A.V. (2008). *Pete's Pathogram.* Lubbock, TX: Action Printing.

Rogers, C. (1980). *A Way of Being.* Boston: Houghton Mifflin.

Tondora, J., Miller, R., & Davidson, L. (2012). "The top ten concerns about person-centered care planning in mental health systems." *The International Journal of Person-Centered Medicine*, 2(3), 410–420.

Wubbolding, R. E. (2000). *Reality Therapy for the 21ˢᵗ Century.* Philadelphia, PA: Brunner Routledge.

Wubbolding, R. E. (2204). *Reverse Paranoia: A World Conspiring to Help You.* Cincinnati, OH: Center for Reality Therapy.

Wubbolding, R. (2011). "Reality therapy: Theories of psychotherapy series." Washington, DC: American Psychological Association.

Wubbolding, R. E. (2015a). "Reality therapy and school practice." In R. Witte & G.S. Mosley-Howard (Eds.), *Mental health practice in today's schools (169–192).* New York, NY: Springer.

Wubbolding, R. E. (2015b). *Reality therapy training manual (16ᵗʰ ed.).* Cincinnati, OH: Center for Reality Therapy.

Wubbolding, R. E. (2016). "Reality therapy." In H. E. A. Tinsley, S. H. Lease, & N. S. Griffin Wiersma (Eds.), *Contemporary Theory and Practice in Counseling and Psychotherapy* (173–200). Los Angeles, CA: Sage.

Wubbolding, R. E. (2017a). *Reality Therapy and Self-Evaluation: The Key to Client Change.* Alexandria, VA: American Counseling Association.

Wubbolding, R. E., Casstevens, W., and Fulkerson, M. H. (2017). "Using the WDEP system of reality therapy to support person-centered treatment planning." *Journal of Counseling & Development*, 95(4), 472–477.

Printed in the United States
By Bookmasters